The Underachieving *Gifted Child*

Recognizing, Understanding, and Reversing Underachievement

Del Siegle, Ph.D.

A CEC-TAG Educational Resource

Cheryll M. Adams, Ph.D., Tracy L. Cross, Ph.D., Susan K. Johnsen, Ph.D., and Diane Montgomery, Ph.D., Series Editors

PRUFROCK PRESS INC.
WACO, TEXAS

Library of Congress Cataloging-in-Publication Data

Siegle, Del.
The underachieving gifted child : recognizing, understanding, and reversing underachievement / by Del Siegle.
  p. cm.
Includes bibliographical references.
ISBN 978-1-59363-956-3 (pbk.)
1. Gifted children--Education--United States. 2. Underachievers--Education--United States. 3. Motivation in education--United States. I. Title.
LC3993.2.S54 2013
371.95--dc23
                    2012022970

Edited by Jennifer Robins

Cover and layout design by Raquel Trevino

ISBN-13: 978-1-59363-956-3

At the time of this book's publication, all facts and figures cited are the most current available. All telephone numbers, addresses, and websites URLs are accurate and active. All publications, organizations, websites, and other resources exist as described in the book, and all have been verified. The author and Prufrock Press Inc. make no warranty or guarantee concerning the information and materials given out by organizations or content found at websites, and we are not responsible for any changes that occur after this book's publication. If you find an error, please contact Prufrock Press Inc.

Prufrock Press Inc.
P.O. Box 8813
Waco, TX 76714-8813
Phone: (800) 998-2208
Fax: (800) 240-0333
http://www.prufrock.com

Table of Contents

Acknowledgments

Much of my understanding of underachievement has been influenced by my research and my life partner, D. Betsy McCoach. This book reflects 13 years of discussions, research, writing, and reading about the topic, and I am indebted to her for her insight and inspiration.

Some of this work was supported by The National Research Center on the Gifted and Talented under the direction of Joseph Renzulli and E. Jean Gubbins. This work was funded through the Educational Research and Development Centers Program, PR/Award Number R206R000001, as administered by the Institute of Education Sciences, U.S. Department of Education. The findings and opinions expressed herein do not reflect the position or policies of the Institute of Education Sciences or the U.S. Department of Education. I wish to acknowledge the contributions of other members of our research team: Sally M. Reis, Meredith Greene Burton, Fredric Schreiber, and Rebecca Mann.

Chapter 7 is reprinted with permission of the The Hong Kong Academy for Gifted Education, Sha Kok Estate, Shatin, N.T., Hong Kong (http://www.hkage.org.hk). It generously allowed me to use material from one of its excellent publications.

I also wish to thank Kelly Shea for her editing and feedback on the initial document, Susan Johnsen at CEC-TAG for suggesting I write this book, and Jennifer Robins at Prufrock Press for her editing skills and incredible patience.

This book is dedicated to the Special Talents Education Program (STEP) students I taught in Glendive, MT. Working with them was a special time in my life, and much of what I know in gifted education I learned from them.

chapter 1

Introduction

> *The greatest achievement of the human spirit is to live up to one's opportunities and make the most of one's resources.*
>
> —Luc de Clapiers

Underachievement is among the most frustrating and bewildering education issues parents and educators face. It is not a crisis of a certain group of people; it is a very real factor in the lives of students from both low and high socioeconomic groups and from rural as well as urban areas. Although it is more common among males, it can also be an issue for females. Underachievement often surfaces around middle school and can continue into high school and beyond (Peterson & Colangelo, 1996). A majority of male underachievers are already underachieving during seventh grade, compared to a majority of female underachievers, who begin to underachieve during eighth and ninth grade (Peterson & Colangelo, 1996). Some researchers have suggested that as high as 50% of gifted students underachieve at some point. However, the extent of underachievement among gifted students is difficult to measure for two reasons. First, there is no universally accepted definition of giftedness. Second, some controversy surrounds what criteria should be used to define underachievement.

On the surface, educators and parents may view academic underachievement as a motivation issue. However, underperforming is much more complex than simply not being motivated. Additionally, several factors contribute to individuals being motivated. Students fail to engage and fail to achieve for a variety of reasons. The purpose of this book is to review the reasons why students are not achieving to their full potential and to discuss strategies that they and others in their environment can consider to help reverse their underachievement.

In the early 1990s, Csikszentmihalyi (1993) coined the term *flow* to describe peak experiences people have. During these experiences, individuals are completely absorbed in what they are doing and often lose track of time. Generally speaking, flow occurs when activities offer a high degree of challenge in areas where individuals perceive themselves as possessing a high degree of skill. Maximum performance occurs during these flow experiences. Flow occurs when individuals have clear goals, decisiveness, the merging of action and awareness, complete (yet effortless) concentration, a sense of control, loss of self-consciousness, an altered sense of time, immediate feedback, and a focus totally on the activity without regard to self (Csikszentmihalyi, 1993). One goal of parents and educators can be to help young people become more engaged so they can have flow experiences. My own work (Siegle & McCoach, 2005b) has shown that students who believe they have the necessary skills to perform a task, who find the task meaningful, and who feel supported in their efforts tend to embrace learning and achieve. Unfortunately, these conditions are often not present for many gifted and talented students in school.

Gentry (Gentry, Rizza, & Gable, 2001) has suggested that five interrelated concepts should underlie educational programs for gifted and talented students: challenge, choice, interest, enjoyment, and personal meaning. Many gifted students are not being academically challenged because they have long ago mastered the content they are being asked to complete (Reis et al., 1993). This is particularly true during the early elementary years. It can be problematic for students because they fail to develop the self-discipline, work habits, and effective study skills that they need once the curriculum does become challenging. A second danger is that they do not come to expect school to be an exciting place for them to grow or to learn new things.

Gifted and talented programs have traditionally focused on identifying students' interests and strengths and providing them with opportunities to explore their passions (Renzulli, 2012). Unfortunately, when economic times are difficult, gifted and talented programs are often the first to be cut (Purcell, 1994). Gifted and talented students also spend the majority of their school experience in the regular classroom where differentiation and choice options are limited (Archambault et al., 1993). Although teachers may want to provide appropriate educational opportunities for the gifted and talented students in their classroom, few teachers have received the necessary training to understand the needs of gifted and talented students and how best to serve them (Archambault et al., 1993).

Educators are not the only group responsible for making school more meaningful for students; parents also play a role. The importance parents place on schoolwork and the type of work ethic they model for their children also directly influence the meaningfulness and enjoyment young people associate with school. Parents who are unhappy with the educational opportunities their gifted and talented offspring is receiving can inadvertently sabotage the child's educational achievement. This is particularly true when parents share their concerns with the student. Parents have a duty to advocate for appropriate educational experiences for their children, but they should also not impugn the importance of school and education.

Although underachievement is not a prominent area of research in general education, it is a major area of concern in gifted education. When The National Research Center on the Gifted and Talented conducted a national needs assessment on issues related to gifted education, the underachievement of gifted students was the highest area of concern (Renzulli, Reid, & Gubbins, 1991). Colangelo (2003) reported that underachievement was the problem most often addressed by counselors in his center for gifted students. In fact, entire careers have been built around counseling and reversing the underachievement patterns of gifted students (Rimm, 1996).

Because humans are diverse and complex beings, decades of research and counseling experiences in the field of gifted education have not produced a single "silver bullet" to solve this perplexing issue. However, promising practices exist, and many individuals have been successful in helping students turn their underachievement around (Baum, Renzulli, & Hébert, 1995; Rimm, 1995; Whitmore, 1980). Underachieving students have traditionally benefitted from counseling interventions, modifications in their curriculum, or a combination of both. What works for one student may not work for another. An individual student may find a topic interesting while another student finds it mundane. What motivates one individual to pursue a challenging course of action holds little relevance to another individual. Although achievers share some central beliefs about themselves and their attitudes to school, underachievers differ much more from each other on these issues (McCoach & Siegle, 2003a). Therefore, no single plan for reversing underachievement works with every student who is not achieving to his or her potential. However, because achievers do share some common characteristics, this information is useful to consider when helping low-achieving students reverse their underachievement pattern.

What we do know is that if nothing is done, many underachievers will not catch up after they leave high school. The greater their underachievement, the less likely they will reverse it. Students with high IQ scores and mediocre grades tend to produce in life what students with average IQ scores and mediocre grades produce. In other words, their life accomplishments are more closely related to their grades than to their academic potential. Their unexplored talents represent potential loss for society and for their own self-fulfillment. However, students with highly educated parents and students with high aspirations have a greater chance of catching up and reversing this pattern (McCall, 1994). Therefore, extra attention needs to be given to students of poverty and students from traditionally underrepresented groups.

So, why do some gifted students fail to perform at a level commensurate with their abilities? What happens to underachieving gifted students in occupational settings if they do not achieve academically during their adolescent years? How can parents and educators help gifted students reach their potential? Can anything be done to reverse underachievement? This book reviews research related to these questions and describes several practices that have helped students recognize their potential and strive to achieve it.

What Is Underachievement?

Who are gifted underachievers? Informally, students whose grades have dropped, who do not complete their homework, or who put off completing projects could certainly be candidates. More formally, controversy surrounds the processes of defining both giftedness and underachievement. Therefore, identifying gifted underachieving students can be difficult for two reasons. First, no universally accepted definition of giftedness exists. Theories of what constitutes giftedness (Sternberg & Davidson, 2005) and what criteria to use in identifying gifted students (Hunsaker, 2012; Johnsen, 2011) abound. However, the field of gifted education has never reached consensus on either a theory or an identification system. Second, disagreement surrounds how to define underachievement. When attempting to identify gifted underachievers, some apply the colloquial expression, "I know it when I see it," a phrase made famous by U.S. Supreme Court Justice Potter Stewart when describing the threshold test for pornography. Similarly, parents with a child who is not performing as expected recognize underachievement without a formal diagnosis. A related issue concerns the value judgment surrounding the term *underachievement*. Whose standards, expectations, or values should be used to determine whether a student is underachieving?

Who Is Gifted?

It is beyond the scope of this book to fully answer the questions, "What is giftedness?" or "Who is gifted?" Readers who are interested in the topic from a theoretical perspective will enjoy reading Sternberg and Davidson's (2005) excellent edited volume, *Conceptions of Giftedness*, or Dai's (2010) text, *The Nature and Nurture of Giftedness*. The National Association for Gifted Children (2010) recently released a position paper on the topic. It provides some guidance for practitioners as they struggle with the concept. I have included the full text of the NAGC position paper in the Appendix. The NAGC definition suggests:

> Gifted individuals are those who demonstrate outstanding levels of aptitude (defined as an exceptional ability to reason and learn) or competence (documented performance or achievement in top 10% or rarer) in one or more domains. Domains include any structured area of activity with its own symbol system (e.g., mathematics, music, language) and/or set of sensorimotor skills (e.g., painting, dance, sports).
>
> The development of ability or talent is a lifelong process. It can be evident in young children as exceptional performance on tests and/or other measures of ability or as a rapid rate of learning, compared to other students of the same age, or in actual achievement in a domain. As individuals mature through childhood to adolescence, however, achievement and high levels of motivation in the domain become the primary characteristics of their giftedness. Various factors can either

enhance or inhibit the development and expression of abilities. (para. 1–2)

For the most part, gifted and talented students in the elementary years are probably those who do things a little earlier and a little better than other students of the same age. They are also those who could be doing things earlier or better if they had been given appropriate opportunities. Many students in this country have not been given appropriate educational opportunities for their giftedness to surface and flourish. This is particularly true for students from underserved populations. These include students of color, students from poverty, and in some cases, students from rural and urban populations.

As students grow older, their advanced abilities become more specialized, and potential is expected to manifest itself. Therefore, gifted underachievers are those who fail to further develop the advanced skills they initially demonstrated or those whose untapped potential failed to materialize. In both cases, it is a discrepancy between what is and what might be. As stated in Chapter 1, it is talent lost—both to the student and to society.

Discrepancy

McCall (1994) suggested that "underachievers do not necessarily have bad grades—just grades not as good as one might expect" (p. 16). This may be particularly true for gifted underachievers. Most definitions of underachievement include a discrepancy between potential (expected performance), often measured by a test, and achievement (actual performance), often measured by achievement tests or school grades (Baum et al., 1995; Dowdall & Colangelo, 1982; Emerick, 1992; Reis & McCoach, 2000; Rimm, 1997; Supplee, 1990; Whitmore, 1980). Practitioners, researchers, and scholars generally agree conceptually that underachievement is a discrepancy between expected and actual performance, but they differ in how they operationalize the discrepancy between potential and performance.

For instance, Emerick (1988) suggested this discrepancy might include any of the following combinations:

- ᔥ high IQ score and low achievement test scores;
- ᔥ high IQ score and low grades;
- ᔥ high achievement test scores and low grades;
- ᔥ high indicators of intellectual, creative potential and low creative productivity; or
- ᔥ high indicators of potential and limited presence of appropriate opportunity for intellectual and creative development.

Emerick's last category is an interesting one. With this definition, others have failed the child by not providing opportunities for his or her talents to manifest themselves. This concern has grown over the past decade as policymakers grapple with the expanding achievement gaps among different groups in the United States (Plucker, Burroughs, & Song, 2010).

The specific students identified by the various discrepancy definitions Emerick (1988) proposed are likely to be quite different from one another. Therefore, lists describing characteristics of underachievers are often contradictory (see Chapter 3). Additionally, a high IQ score and low achievement test scores may indicate the presence of a learning disability, whereas high achievement test scores and low grades seldom indicate a learning disability. Educators and parents must be careful not to immediately assume a bright child who is having difficulty in school is underachieving; the student may have a learning disability. Moon and Hall (1998) have suggested that gifted students who are underachieving should be screened for a learning disability. The first step in Sylvia Rimm's Trifocal Model (see Chapter 6) is a comprehensive assessment of the student's strengths and abilities; this assessment should reveal any learning disabilities a student might have.

There are several issues that one must consider when defining underachievement using a discrepancy between expected achievement and actual achievement. First, how should one determine expected achievement? Second, how should one determine a student's actual achievement? Third, how severe must the discrepancy be between expected achievement and actual achievement?

Measuring Expected Achievement

Ability measures such as IQ tests are traditionally used to determine levels of expected achievement. In fact, underachievement first became an educational issue in the mid-1950s as a result of the broad acceptance of ability and achievement tests (McCall, 1994). Once the public gained confidence in the use of these tests, concerns began to surface about students who were not performing at the level the tests predicted they should. Ability and achievement are substantially correlated; however, the degree of this relation is far from perfect. The correlation between ability and achievement is approximately .80 (Deary, Strand, Smith, & Fernandes, 2007). Although this correlation is quite strong, it leaves 36% of the fluctuation in achievement unaccounted for by ability. For example, *conscientiousness*, one of the Big Five personality traits—*emotional stability, extroversion, agreeableness*, and *openness* being the others—correlates with college GPA and has also been shown to be largely independent of intelligence. Agreeableness and openness are also related to achievement, but their relationship disappears once statistical models account for intelligence (Poropat, 2009). Therefore, many factors, including personality, play a role in student achievement. Still, achievement tests are widely used in schools across the country and are readily available, which makes them an excellent source of information.

Students with learning disabilities often score higher on tests of cognitive ability than they do on standardized achievement tests. This is particularly true for students with reading disabilities, because IQ tests require less reading than standardized achievement tests. As stated earlier, students with high ability and low standardized achievement test scores may be underachievers, or they may have undiagnosed learning disabilities and should be screened for learning disabilities prior to treating them for underachievement. For the above reasons, Siegle and McCoach (in press) recommended that standardized achievement tests provide a better indicator of expected achievement than intelligence tests do. Care must be taken to ensure the achievement test does not have a ceiling that limits its ability to measure the extent of the student's advanced skills. An out-of-level test should be used if this occurs.

Measuring Actual Achievement

Given the definition of underachievement as a discrepancy between expected achievement and actual achievement, standardized achievement test scores are not appropriate measures of actual student achievement for two reasons. First, if standardized achievement test scores are used to determine a student's expected achievement, they cannot also be used to measure the student's actual achievement. Second, standardized test scores are not a good indicator of a student's classroom performance, and classroom performance is a good indicator of later success in life (McCall, Evahn, & Kratzler, 1992). McCall et al. (1992) conducted the largest longitudinal study of underachievers to date and documented the role classroom grades play in future productivity. Thirteen years after high school, the educational and occupational status of high school underachievers paralleled their grades in high school rather than their abilities. In other words, students with high IQ scores and mediocre grades performed similarly to students with average IQ scores and mediocre grades. As mentioned in Chapter 1, McCall (1994) has suggested that students are more likely to catch up in life if their parents are well educated and the students have high aspirations.

Classroom grades provide the most valid indication of a student's level of achievement within a classroom. However, using classroom grades to assess academic achievement also poses problems. We cannot equate grades across teachers, classes, and schools. Even within the same school, instructors teaching the same course may have very different methods for assigning grades. Many teachers consider factors other than academic achievement (i.e., effort and behavior) when assigning grades (Marzano, 2000). Therefore, comparing grades or GPAs across students can be misleading. Given these drawbacks, my colleagues and I (Siegle & McCoach, in press) still believe grades are the best reflection of how a student is performing in a given class and of student motivation. In fact, underachievement tends to show up when students begin encountering teachers who assign challenging assignments and require homework (McCall, 1994).

Therefore, a possible yardstick to measure underachievement is the discrepancy between students' achievement scores and their grades. These students are apparently learning the material but are not producing in their classrooms. Most of this book centers on these students and addresses the motivation issues surrounding this phenomenon. Unfortunately, chronic underachievers who have underachieved for an extended period of time may begin to demonstrate mediocre or low achievement test scores and mediocre or poor grades as a result of disengaged classroom performance over multiple years. An improvement in motivation for these students must be accompanied by academic remediation to correct deficit skills that they possess after years of underachievement.

Severity of the Discrepancy Between Expected and Actual Achievement

Reis and McCoach (2000) published a comprehensive review of the literature on gifted underachievers and proposed the following definition:

> Underachievers are students who exhibit a severe discrepancy between *expected achievement* (as measured by standardized achievement test scores or cognitive or intellectual ability assessments) and *actual achievement* (as measured by class grades and teacher evaluations). To be classified as an underachiever, the discrepancy between expected and actual achievement must not be the direct result of a diagnosed learning disability and must persist over an extended period of time. Gifted underachievers are underachievers who exhibit superior scores on measures of expected achievement (i.e., standardized achievement test scores or cognitive or intellectual ability assessments). (p. 157)

How severe should the discrepancy be between expected achievement and actual achievement before a student is considered underachieving? First, given the phenomenon of regression to the mean, we would not expect the actual achievement levels of those with the highest standardized achievement to be equally extreme. Regression to the mean is a phenomenon where extremely high or extremely low scores tend to move toward the average on later or related testing simply by chance. For example, a student who earns a perfect score on a test is likely not to have a second perfect score because he or she might misread a question or have some other chance error occur. Similarly, a student who misses every question might by chance answer one or two correctly on a second or different test. In addition to the possibility of regression to the mean, most people probably perform somewhat below their capacity or ability, so some discrepancy is expected. Thus, the discrepancy between students' expected achievement and their actual achievement must be severe enough to warrant substantial concern. The discrepancy also must be chronic. Patterns of underachievement must persist long enough to be detectable and to cause adverse consequences. In other words, we would not consider a child an underachiever who traditionally earned A's in mathematics, but suddenly earned a C. If those C's continued for several marking periods, then parents and educators should become concerned. Care must be taken to ensure that episodic underachievement does not morph into ongoing underachievement.

For those who like numbers and statistics, McCall (1994) suggested that students who fall more than one standard error below the regression of grades on an ability measure represent an acceptable statistical discrepancy. He argued that this definition holds well across different samples and with different measures of potential and performance. It also works well across different levels of ability and grades. As a hypothetical example, assume students with IQ scores of 130 have a predicted grade point average (GPA) of 3.6, and students with IQ scores of 100 have a predicted GPA of 2.9. If the standard error were .43, students with an IQ of 130 who earn a 2.5 GPA would fall more than one standard error (.43) below the predicted GPA of 3.6, and students with an IQ of 100 who earned a 2.5 would just avoid falling one standard error (.43) below their predicted GPA (2.9).

Selective Achievement

Before I conclude this chapter, I need to address the issue of *selective achievement*. Some have argued (Delisle & Galbraith, 2002; Hébert, 2011; Porter, 2005) that students who choose to put their energies into areas other than school should not be labeled underachievers, and the label of underachievement is often a value judgment.

> Labeling a student an underachiever requires making a value judgment about the worthiness of certain accomplishments. A teacher may believe that reading *Huckleberry Finn* is more worthwhile than mastering a new video game, but a child may not. This behavior illustrates a value conflict between adults and child. (Reis & McCoach, 2000, p. 156)

On a personal note, I was one of the taller boys in my high school, and some thought I should be playing basketball. I had poor eyesight and lacked depth perception. I had no interest in playing basketball; the last activity I wanted to pursue was one that involved fast-moving flying objects. I elected not to participate in basketball, much to the anguish of an older cousin. Some might classify me as an underachieving basketball player. Had I been a foot taller, more might have classified me as such. This brings us to an interesting point—underachieving in whose eyes? It is unreasonable to expect gifted students to achieve at the highest levels in every area. Gifted students may choose not to exert effort in areas that are not important to them while expending effort to excel in areas that they enjoy and value. This is generally referred to as selective achievement. Additionally, each student possesses a unique spectrum of traits and talents. Therefore, even highly gifted students may perform at near-average levels in an area of relative weakness.

In addition to selective achievement, some have proposed the term *nonproducer*. From this perspective, students are simply electing not to do the work others may be asking them to do. As with selective achievement, the choice to be engaged is with the student. These situations are similar to life outside school. Ultimately, the final decision about what each of us pursues is up to us. However, there is an additional twist with gifted underachievers. For some nonproducing individuals, having the label of gifted is sufficiently satisfying: "It doesn't matter whether I have accomplished anything, I'm still gifted." As I travel across the country, I often find myself seated on airplanes next to a 40–50-year-old gifted nonproducer. These nonproducers lament the fact that they haven't developed their talents and reached their potential. However, they seem to bask in the afterglow of the gifted label or high-IQ score they received as a child. Subotnik, Olszewski-Kubilius, and Worrell (2011) cautioned that although general abilities are often associated with giftedness at a young age, as students grow older, their domain-specific abilities become more important. One could make the case, although not universally accepted, that these individuals are no longer gifted underachievers. They simply are average or below-average achievers. The area of adult underachievement is one that has received little attention and is beyond the scope of this book. I will focus our attention on young people who could be doing better.

Thus, the students who should be of greatest concern are those who are failing to achieve in *any* productive area over a period of time. As Peterson (2001) cautioned, "Wise educators will not make judgments about future prospects for underachievers based on only one stage of development or during a time of significant personal or family transition" (p. 246). For example, even successful gifted students may experience uneven academic performance from time to time in high school. The difference between them and underachievers is that they have established habits of achievement that are able to withstand academic unevenness (Peterson & Colangelo, 1996).

As Warnemuende and Samson (1991) noted, "Although we call the child an underachiever, remember, underachievement is not a diagnosis. It is not the primary problem. It is a symptom or sign that there is a problem which results in underachievement" (pp. 9–10). In the next chapter, I will discuss the characteristics and behaviors of someone with this problem. Beginning with Chapter 4, I will share possible reasons for underachievement and provide promising strategies to address it.

Characteristics of Underachievers

On the surface, describing the characteristics of underachievers seems like a simple task. However, just as there are no definitive definitions of giftedness or underachievement, there is no universal set of characteristics that all underachievers share. Each student is somewhat unique and exhibits a unique combination of behaviors. Having said this, there do appear to be patterns, and several practitioners and researchers (Heacox, 1991; Mandel & Marcus, 1988; Rimm, 1995; Siegle & McCoach, 2005a) have proposed different types of underachievers. Based on these types, factors commonly associated with underachievement include:

- ❧ low academic self-perceptions (Freedman, 2000; Matthews & McBee, 2007; Supplee, 1990; Whitmore, 1980);
- ❧ low self-efficacy (Siegle & McCoach, 2005b);
- ❧ low self-motivation and low effort toward academic tasks (Albaili, 2003; Baslanti & McCoach, 2006; Lacasse,

1999; Matthews & McBee, 2007; McCoach & Siegle, 2003b; Rayneri, Gerber, & Wiley, 2003; Weiner, 1992);

‰ external attributions (Carr, Borkowski, & Maxwell, 1991; Siegle & McCoach, 2005b);

‰ low goal valuation (Baslanti & McCoach, 2006; Freedman, 2000; Lacasse, 1999; Matthews & McBee, 2007; McCall et al., 1992; McCoach & Siegle, 2003b);

‰ negative attitude toward school and teachers (Colangelo, Kerr, Christensen, & Maxey, 1993; Ford, 1996; McCoach & Siegle, 2003b; Rimm, 1995); and

‰ low self-regulatory or metacognitive skills (Carr et al., 1991; Krouse & Krouse, 1981; Yu, 1996).

Although many underachievers exhibit deficits in one or more of the characteristics listed above, very few underachievers display low levels on all of these characteristics. They appear to be a fairly diverse group. We must remember that some underachievers may not exhibit deficits in any of these areas. Therefore, the variability of motivational and attitudinal measures within samples of underachievers tends to be higher than the variability for comparison groups of average or high achievers. For example, groups of gifted underachievers display significantly more variability on self-report measures of motivation, perceptions, and attitudes than gifted achievers do (McCoach & Siegle, 2003a). The large amount of variability suggests that although underachievers may share some common characteristics, they are not a homogeneous population of students. Each student may underachieve for a somewhat unique reason or combination of reasons; therefore, it is possible that gifted underachievers may be low on only one or two of the many characteristics commonly ascribed to underachievers and may be average or even well above average in all other areas. This variability among gifted underachievers is one of the reasons reversing student underachievement is such a perplexing issue.

Given the variability among underachievers, as previously stated, several researchers and practitioners in the area of underachievement have proposed specific subtypes of underachievers (e.g., Heacox, 1991; Mandel & Marcus, 1988, 1995; Rimm, 1995, 1997; Siegle

& McCoach, 2005b). Each of these types might require a different intervention strategy. Table 1 shows the different types of underachievers that various researchers and practitioners have proposed and how these different types overlap from one researcher to another. The underachievers cluster into 17 different types. Some research suggests that underachieving gifted students share more common characteristics with underachievers in general than they do with achieving gifted students (Dowdall & Colangelo, 1982; McCall et al., 1992).

Parents, teachers, and counselors play an important role in identifying and working with gifted underachievers. Naturally, parents observe their children's progress on a daily basis, so they are often the first to realize that a child's achievement has begun to decline. Parents are also able to recognize changes in their children's attitudes toward school and learning.

Because teachers and counselors have ready access to student files, they may be able to identify clues to early difficulties gifted students might be experiencing. Information about behaviors, achievement, course selection, attendance, and tardiness can be used to identify students early enough so that prevention of underachievement can occur as opposed to remediation for underachievement. For example, gifted underachievers miss more school, are more often tardy, and select fewer demanding electives than gifted achievers (Peterson & Colangelo, 1996). Unfortunately, by high school, teachers may be unaware that chronically underachieving students were ever considered "gifted." Long-term academic underachievers may have knowledge and skills deficits and may show no signs of intellectual promise in the classroom.

Educators who do the detective work to find these hidden students who were formerly identified as gifted may be able to work with the teachers, parents, and students to tap into students' strengths and interests. They may also be able to provide individual and/or group counseling to help these underachievers to become more successful students. Counselors can also provide test data that document the gifted students' academic functioning level. In some cases, this information is in the student file, but sometimes it may be necessary to test students with out-of-level tests to determine exactly where they are

Table 1 Types of Underachievers

Researcher	Description
Mandel & Marcus: Coasting Underachiever **Rimm:** Passive Paul (Dependent Conformer) **Heacox:** The Complacent Learner	These students demonstrate a lack of concern for their schoolwork and are content to slip by with poor or mediocre grades. They often procrastinate, are easily distracted, and turn assignments in late. Any attempt by these students to improve their grades or to work harder is often short-lived.
Mandel & Marcus: Anxious Underachiever **Rimm:** Perfectionist Pearl (Dependent Conformer) **Heacox:** The Stressed Learner	Characterized by a fear of failure, these students are tense and self-conscious. They rely on structure and organization and may have difficulty with abstract thought or open-ended assignments. Because they set unrealistic expectations for themselves, they will sometimes avoid attempting an assignment for fear of failing or making a mistake.
Mandel & Marcus: Defiant Underachiever **Rimm:** Rebellious Rebecca (Dominant Non-Conformer) **Heacox:** The Rebel	These students view school as pointless, and they will let others know this by acting out and defying authority figures. They are often spiteful and angry and can lose their temper quickly.
Mandel & Marcus: Sad and Depressed Underachiever **Rimm:** Depressed Donna (Dependent Non-Conformer)	These students display the symptoms of depression, including low energy and self-esteem, feelings of sadness and hopelessness, disrupted sleeping and eating patterns, and a lack of concentration. They are often unable or unwilling to focus on their schoolwork.
Mandel & Marcus: Identity Search Underachiever **Rimm:** Creative Chris (Dominant Non-Conformer)	These students are very passionate individuals who do not want to conform. They question the existing structure and values of society, and argue about the importance of school, their classes, and the work they are assigned.
Mandel & Marcus: Wheeler-Dealer Underachiever **Rimm:** Manipulative Maria (Dominant Non-Conformer)	These students are insecure in their self-concepts and will take advantage of family, teachers, and other students in order to obtain their way. They value their social lives more than their academic lives, but their social circle is often unstable.
Rimm: Social Sally, Jock Jack, Dramatic Dan (Dominant Conformers) **Heacox:** The Conformist	Characterized by social successes, these students choose to participate in the social or extracurricular, competitive activities in which they know they will excel. They fear that they will be labeled "nerds" if they demonstrate academic ability, so they underachieve to avoid being alienated by their peer group.
Rimm: Poor Polly (Dependent Conformer) **Heacox:** The Victim	These students seek validation from authority figures to boost their low self-esteem. They feel sorry for themselves and are dependent on family and teachers for help and reassurance.

Table 1, continued

Researcher	Description
Rimm: Torn Tomas **Heacox:** The Distracted Learner	Personal factors outside of the school environment affect these students' academic performance. These students either are experiencing or have experienced a traumatic event, or simply have multiple responsibilities and commitments outside of the classroom. Compared to these external factors, schoolwork is not as important to these students.
Heacox: The Bored Student	These students will avoid their schoolwork, claiming it is boring. They may not be properly challenged by school activities, or they may be using boredom as an excuse to cover for their fear of failure.
Heacox: The Struggling Student	These students may lack the study and time management skills needed for success. Either they were able to successfully achieve without much effort in earlier grades and so never developed those skills, or they may suffer from a mild learning disability that is not deemed severe enough to require special services.
Heacox: The Single-Sided Achiever	Characterized by a focused interest and/or talent in a single subject, these students may only achieve in certain classes or for certain teachers. They neglect other areas of study and talent development, electing to underachieve in those areas that do not align with their primary interests.
Rimm: Hyperactive Harry	These children are inconsistent in their work and behavior. They are often impulsive and disorganized and may frequently touch or bother other students.
Rimm: Academic Alice	Originally high achievers, these students shut down when they cannot meet their own high expectations. After a few failed attempts to live up to their previous performances, these students experience a significant drop in their self-efficacy and self-esteem. They may choose to underachieve because they feel they are incapable of anything else.
Rimm: Taunted Terris (Dependent Non-Conformer)	These students are bullied and victimized in school. They have low self-esteem and may feel helpless or useless. They rely on parents and other authority figures to protect, help, and support them.
Rimm: Sick Sam (Dependent Non-Conformer)	These students may fake an illness to avoid attending school or completing their schoolwork. The illnesses may be entirely fabricated, or they may be psychosomatic if the student is anxious about attending school for any reason.
Rimm: Bully Bob (Dominant Non-Conformer)	These students are aggressive, rebellious, and lose their tempers easily. They view school and schoolwork as pointless and will lash out at authority figures when things are not going their way. These students normally do not have many friends because they pick on and bully the other students.

functioning. Many gifted students' achievement levels are underestimated because the students are performing beyond the test ceiling for their current grade level.

Gender

Studies over the last half-century suggest that gifted males underachieve at two to three times the rate of gifted females (Baker, Bridger, & Evans, 1998; Gowan, 1955; Matthews & McBee, 2007; McCall, 1994; McCoach, 2002; McCoach & Siegle, 2001; Peterson & Colangelo, 1996; Richert, 1991; Siegle, Reis, & McCoach, 2006). Although gifted males tend to outperform gifted females on off-level mathematics and science subtests, and females outperform males on verbal subtests (Olszewski-Kubilius & Lee, 2011), females still tend to have higher high school GPAs than males (Cole, 1997; Duckworth & Seligman, 2006). Males and females as a group appear to show strengths in different domains, yet females are outperforming males in classroom work without regard to the domain. Recent data indicate that the underachievement boys are experiencing in school is following them beyond school. Females are entering and graduating from college in greater numbers with higher GPAs than males (Conger & Long, 2010; Sheard, 2009). Using the 2008 U.S. Census Bureau data, James Chung of Reach Advisors found that women ages 22–30 with no husband and no children earn 8% more than comparable men in the top 366 metropolitan areas (Luscombe, 2010). Better education accounts for much of the gain. Not having children is also a factor. Overall, wage differences between females and males have not disappeared. However, young, educated females without children are currently earning more than their male counterparts.

Boys appear to value some school subjects less than girls. Siegle and Reis (1998) reported that gifted boys and girls in middle school saw mathematics, science, and social studies as being equally important, but boys not only believed language arts was less important than females believed it was, but boys also felt they had less ability in language arts than girls. For several decades, educators have been concerned about the limited number of women pursuing STEM (science, technology, engineering, and mathematics) careers. Although this continues to be an issue that educators and parents need to address, evidence is mounting that similar efforts are needed to promote the importance of language arts for males.

As noted before, grade 7 appears to be critical for male students, while grades 8 and 9 are more critical for female students. Because females display the types of behaviors that are rewarded in classrooms and their underachievement starts later than boys (Peterson & Colangelo, 1996), it is possible that their underachievement is being overlooked. Educators should therefore pay attention to bright females who are doing average work. Some of these females may be gifted underachievers who could be doing better. Male students are also more likely than female students to be extreme underachievers, so they are also more likely to be identified. However, it is equally plausible based on records of school grades that the 2:1 or 3:1 ratio of gifted male underachievers to gifted female underachievers actually exists.

Peers

Peers can positively or negatively affect students' achievement. Reis, Hébert, Diaz, Maxfield, and Ratley (1995) found that high-achieving peers had a positive influence on students who were beginning to underachieve. These high-achieving peers contributed to some students' reversal of underachievement. In a national longitudinal study of secondary students (NELS:88), students with friends who cared about learning showed better educational outcomes than those in less educationally oriented peer groups (Chen, 1997).

However, peers can also have a negative impact. Clasen and Clasen (1995) found that 66% of high-achieving students reported peer pressure, and the attitude of other students, including friends, was a primary force in not earning good grades. Coleman and Cross (2005), in a discussion of coping with giftedness and standing out, noted, "in adolescence, it becomes a greater problem for the studiously inclined gifted child because intellectual pursuits become less acceptable to peers" (p. 168).

Young people who underachieve tend to have peers who underachieve. Berndt (1999) found that students' grades were more closely related to their friends' grades at the end of the school year than at the beginning, and students' grades decreased from fall to spring if their friends had lower grades in the fall. As early as fourth and fifth grade, students affiliate with others who share their motivation patterns, and they reorganize their peer groups as the year progresses to preserve these motivation patterns (Kindermann, 1993).

Siegle and McCoach (in press) noted, "although peer achievement levels do relate to students' academic achievement, it is unclear whether the choice to associate with other non-achievers is a cause or a result of gifted students' underachievement" (p. 893).

Family Dynamics

Although there is limited empirical research on the family characteristics of underachieving gifted students, what exists suggests that certain types of home environments may be related to the development of students' achievement and underachievement patterns (Baker et al., 1998; Brown, Mounts, Lamborn, & Steinberg, 1993; Rimm & Lowe, 1988; Zilli, 1971). Inconsistent parenting techniques appear to occur more frequently in the homes of underachieving children (Rimm & Lowe, 1988). Parents of underachievers tend to be either overly lenient or overly strict (Pendarvis, Howley, & Howley, 1990; Weiner, 1992), or may vacillate between lenient and strict. In addition, bestowing adult status on a child at too young an age may contribute to the development of underachievement (Fine & Pitts, 1980; Rimm & Lowe, 1988).

In a qualitative study of gifted urban underachievers, the family dysfunction that characterized the lives of the gifted underachievers contrasted the happier home lives of the gifted achievers (Reis et al., 1995). Conversely, another study comparing the families of underachievers and achievers found that families with underachieving gifted students were not any more likely to be dysfunctional than families with achieving gifted students (Green, Fine, & Tollefson, 1988). However, dysfunctional families with achieving gifted students reported greater satisfaction with their family lives than did dysfunctional families of underachieving students. Regardless of their achievement status, functional families were more satisfied with their adolescents' academic achievement than were dysfunctional families. The question becomes, "Does the underachievement of the child create problems in the family unit, do students underachieve because they come from families in conflict, or is there a dynamic interaction between the underachiever and the family?"

Students do well in school when they have a supportive academic home climate that meshes with the academic climate in their schools. The academic home climate fosters beliefs, attitudes, and motivation that lead to higher achievement (Campbell & Verna, 2007). Parents can teach their children to foster adaptability and accept school responsibilities. Parents can establish good working relationships with teachers and help their children develop a respect for authority. Parents help their students when they are supportive of school and monitor schoolwork. For example, parents may show their children how to do homework but not do it for them. Parents should emphasize the importance of setting high expectations and accepting challenges. They can instill work habits at early stages of their children's school career. They can emphasize communication skills and promote sociability. Parents of achieving students also generate curiosity and encourage their children to pursue their academic interests.

Garn, Matthews, and Jolly (2010) found that about half of the parents of gifted children they interviewed viewed themselves as having a better grasp on their children's needs than their children's teachers. They found parents de-emphasized teacher authority in favor of parent oversight and control. This can be problematic for student achievement. Because of this, the researchers suggested that schools need to reach out to parents on a consistent basis to facilitate open communication about personalized motivational strategies that parents and teachers view as effective for student achievement. Counselors can play a key role in facilitating these discussions.

Poverty and Underserved Populations

Underachievement can occur when gifted students do not receive the support and educational services they require to develop their talent. Gifted students of poverty and students from underserved groups are particularly vulnerable. Students who are not given adequate opportunities to develop their talents often become *involuntary underachievers*. Forty-four percent of lower income students who enter first grade in the top 10% will not score in the top 10% by the time they reach fifth grade (Wyner, Bridgeland, & DiIulio, 2007). Gifted students from higher income homes progress twice as fast as their gifted peers from lower income homes. "In elementary and high school, *lower-income students neither maintain their status as high achievers nor rise into the ranks of high achievers as frequently as higher-income students*" (Wyner et al., 2007, p. 5, italics in original). High-achieving, lower income students drop out of high school or do not graduate on time at a rate twice that of their higher income peers. They are less likely to graduate from college than their higher income peers and less likely to attend the most selective colleges. Limited resources in their schools, communities, and families factor into the involuntary underachievement of many students from underserved populations.

Culturally diverse students also face unique barriers to their achievement for several reasons. Minority students are often underrepresented in programs for the gifted and talented (Ford, 1996; Tomlinson, Callahan, & Lelli, 1997) and overrepresented in special education (Ladner & Hammons, 2001). Culturally diverse students continue to face unintentional bias at school and in society at large (Ford, 1996). Further, the definition of achievement in a particular subculture may be very different from that of the dominant culture.

Students' attitudes toward school (Ford, 1996) and the relationship they see between school and their future success and prosperity

(Sanders, 1998) influence their academic achievement. Unfortunately, students of poverty may not see positive options for their future. Sanders (1998) found that Black students valued education when they saw it as a means to a better economic situation. However, they were less positive about the importance of education when they did not see it as a means to an improved economic situation. I will discuss the important role meaningfulness plays in achievement in Chapter 9.

One caution before I conclude our discussion of characteristics of underachievers: Although the topic of this book is underachievement, labeling a student as an underachiever is a harsh judgment. I use the term throughout this book, but I caution readers to avoid the label with students. Each of us is a work in progress, and who we are today is not who we will be in the future. My goal with the remainder of this book is to address some of the reasons gifted students may not be performing at levels their parents and teachers might expect and to provide some suggestions to increase these students' motivation and promote the natural love of learning that children possess when they first enter the world.

chapter 4

Dweck's Mindsets
Recognizing Effort and Ability

Everyone has the potential to become smarter than they are now.
—Carol Dweck

Addressing Students' Giftedness

A common concern among educators and parents is how to talk with young people about being gifted. How parents and teachers talk with students about their giftedness can actually have positive and negative effects on their motivation and achievement. As we interact with gifted children, we walk a fine line between recognizing the outstanding ability behind their gifts and talents and promoting the importance of effort and hard work in developing those gifts. Students who have been identified as gifted and talented obviously have demonstrated advanced behaviors that have caused others to recognize their giftedness. In this chapter, I will discuss how we can recognize the outstanding talents young people demonstrate while helping them understand the important role effort plays in high levels of performance. A key component of many gifted students' underachievement is their failure to understand the important role effort and hard work play in developing their talents. An important step in reversing underachievement is helping students understand what it means to be gifted and the relationship between ability and effort. This conversation should begin when students are first identified as gifted and talented.

One inclination may be to avoid addressing the issue of being gifted. However, not addressing students' identification as gifted may actually influence the development of students' mindsets. When educators and parents fail to talk with students about their talents and how they acquired them, students are left to draw their own conclusions about the innateness or malleability of the skills they possess.

If students are not already aware that they have some special abilities, they will be once they have been identified as gifted and start participating in educational opportunities that differ from what their peers are experiencing. They will also recognize that their classmates in the advanced classes they attend appear to be very "smart." Therefore, the significance and implications of being gifted need to be addressed. As we discuss giftedness with students, we can strike a balance between recognizing the students' giftedness—the skills that led to their identification—and helping them recognize the importance of effort in continuing to develop their talents. Our goal is to encourage what Carol Dweck calls a *growth mindset*.

Mindset Theory

Dweck (2012) has researched and written extensively on the importance of having a growth mindset. She has stressed the importance of students seeing talents and abilities as dynamic and malleable qualities. She noted that students who see their intelligence as something that can be developed, rather than simply a fixed trait, are more motivated to learn, persevere more in the face of obstacles, are more resilient after setbacks, and ultimately achieve more. However, Aronson and Juarez (2012) have cautioned that having an attitude and actually using it may be different matters. They suggested that whether students believe intelligence is malleable or fixed predicts very little about individuals' performance on many tests. It appears that students' attitudes toward intelligence must be activated. Extensive research by Dweck and others has shown that intensive interventions can activate attitudes and do actually lift grades, test scores, and engagement. According to Aronson and Juarez, these interventions probably work because they turn attitudes into growth mindsets upon which individuals act.

Mindset Theory and Giftedness

We are only beginning to explore Dweck's theory as it relates to the field of gifted and talented education. The foundation of gifted education is based on recognizing students' interests and strengths (Renzulli, 2012). It is also based on recognizing ability. Subotnik et al. (2011) noted, "General intellectual ability and specific abilities such as mathematical cast of mind, spatial ability, physical memory, or musicality predict and are fundamental prerequisites for high achievement and eminence in their respective fields" (p. 39). Mindset theory does not require educators and parents to ignore individual differences. As Dweck (2012) has noted, individuals do not necessarily need to believe that everyone has the same intelligence or that anyone can accomplish anything; however, they must "believe that everyone has the potential to become smarter than they are now" (p. 8). Other researchers (Buschkuehl, Jaeggi, Shah, & Jonides, 2012; Diamond, 2012; Pakulak & Neville, 2012) have documented the brain's plasticity and provide support for individuals' potential for growth.

Dweck (2012) suggested that educators of the gifted carefully consider how they portray giftedness to students and how they encourage students who excel. This is particularly relevant for students who are identified for and benefit from gifted and talented programs. Past research (Heller & Ziegler, 1996, 2001; McNabb, 2003; Siegle & Reis, 1998) has suggested that students who are identified as gifted and talented tend to attribute their successes more to ability than effort. Such beliefs are commonly associated with a fixed mindset.

Students with a fixed mindset believe abilities are innate and cannot be changed, a belief that is associated with an entity theory of intelligence. The adage "You cannot teach an old dog new tricks" reflects this mindset. Students with a growth mindset, however, see abilities as malleable. This belief is associated with an incremental theory of intelligence. The adage "Practice makes perfect" reflects this mindset (see Chapter 5 for issues related to perfectionism).

Murphy and Dweck (2010) found individuals within an organization will adopt the mindset that they perceive is prevalent within that organization. Accordingly, gifted students who believe that their teachers or schools hold an entity theory of intelligence will more likely display behaviors associated with that entity theory, such as bragging about a test score or their IQ. Therefore, the ways in which parents and teachers talk with students about their selection for gifted services and the mindsets parents and teachers hold, as well as the ways they encourage students who excel, contribute to students' mindsets.

Dweck (1999) demonstrated that students who believe abilities can be developed and are not fixed are more likely to attempt challenging tasks and persevere through difficulties than students who believe abilities are innate. Students who have a fixed mindset approach new situations as opportunities to show what they know. Therefore, they may view any mistakes as evidence they lack ability. This can be a significant handicap in the challenging classes typically offered in gifted education. In contrast, students who have a growth mindset view new situations as opportunities to acquire new skills or improve their existing skills. They are more likely to tackle difficult tasks in order to become smarter. Although Dweck (1999) found that students already gravitate toward one or the other of these orientations in elementary school, she also found that these orientations are amenable to change, so parents' and teachers' roles should be to encourage a growth mindset.

Developmental Theories of Giftedness

Joseph Renzulli and Françoys Gagné are two theorists in gifted education whose work fits well with the growth mindset that Dweck has proposed. Renzulli (2005) has preferred to label the behavior rather than the student. Instead of saying a particular child is gifted, he has recommended that the behaviors the student is displaying be labeled. For him, gifted is an adjective, and he suggests that giftedness is brought to bear upon some performance area. In his Three Ring Conception of Giftedness (see Figure 1), giftedness is a behavior that comes to fruition in certain (but not all) students, at certain times (but not all of the time), and under certain circumstances. Giftedness is something students do, not something they are. According to Renzulli, giftedness occurs when students are task committed and use their above-average ability in creative ways.

Gagné (2005) distinguished between the terms gifted and talented; gifts are the raw material, and talents are the byproduct of developing that material. In his Differentiated Model of Giftedness and Talent (see Figure 2), individuals turn their gifts into talents. This transformation occurs through the interaction of a developmental process, catalysts (such as the environment and intrapersonal characteristics), and chance. Both theories follow a developmental perspective that is compatible with mindset theory.

These developmental theorists proposed that students have something to do with their giftedness. Giftedness is not something that *just happens* to students. Certainly some students are able to learn material more quickly or earlier than other students, and some students are also able to grasp more complex and complicated ideas better than others. However, these advantages are not sufficient to predict long-term differences in success later in life. As Geoff Colvin (2008) wrote in *Talent Is Overrated*, "talents are much less important than we think" (p. 35). What makes a difference in the long term is the deliberate practice that students embrace. Deliberate practice is practice that focuses on tasks beyond students' current level of comfort and competence. It requires feedback from a knowledgeable coach who

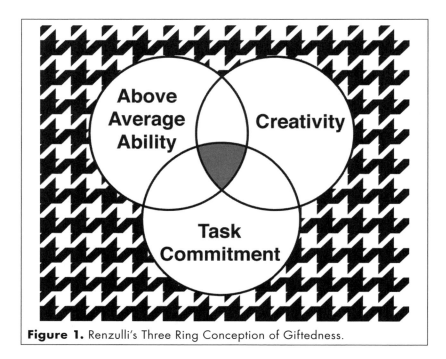

Figure 1. Renzulli's Three Ring Conception of Giftedness.

can guide them through the process and also help them learn how to coach themselves (Ericsson, Prietula, & Cokely, 2007). It requires a growth mindset that understands that abilities are malleable and can be improved with concentrated effort. It also takes time to develop giftedness and reach a high level of expertise. Although domains of talent have unique developmental trajectories across the life span, it generally takes a minimum of 10,000 hours of deliberate practice over 10 years to achieve expertise (Ericsson et al., 2007; Subotnik et al., 2011). Obviously, giftedness is not something that just happens to individuals.

As stated earlier, research interventions to activate a growth mindset abound in the research literature; however, most research has not specifically examined these strategies with students who have been identified as gifted and talented. Burns and Isbell (2007) warned, "when considering the use of a malleability intervention, researchers should consider the skill level of their participants, as well as their self-

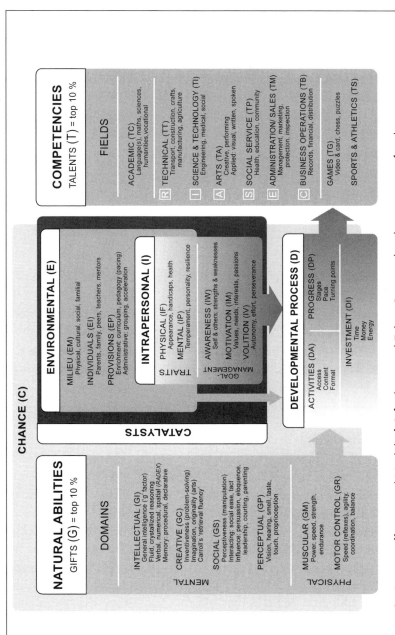

Figure 2. Gagné Differentiated Model of Giftedness and Talent. Reprinted with permission of author.

theories" (p. 61). In their exploratory study of this issue, they found that contradictory mindsets reacted differently depending on the skill level of the participants. They found that priming individuals for a malleability mindset worked better for individuals with an incremental theory of intelligence who were moderately skilled in mathematics than for those who were highly skilled in mathematics. Conversely, priming a fixedness mindset was more useful for individuals with an entity theory of intelligence who were highly skilled in mathematics than for those who were moderately skilled. As Aronson and Juarez (2012) noted, an entity theory of intelligence may actually reinforce positive expectations and self-esteem with highly skilled students and propel them to heightened performances.

Self-Efficacy

A related issue is student self-efficacy, which will be discussed further in Chapter 8. Self-efficacy refers to an individual's judgment about being able to perform a particular activity. It is an individual's "I can" or "I can't" belief. Stanford University professor Albert Bandura (1977) first introduced the construct of self-efficacy in the late 1970s. Research during the past 30 years has revealed a positive relationship between self-efficacy beliefs and academic performance and persistence (Martin & Marsh, 2006; Multon, Brown, & Lent, 1991; Skaalvik & Skaalvik, 2004). The relationship exists across a wide variety of subjects, experimental designs, and assessment methods. Those with high self-efficacy are not only more likely to attempt new tasks, but also work harder and persist longer in the face of difficulties (Bandura, 1986; Lyman, Prentice-Dunn, Wilson, & Bonfilio, 1984; Multon et al., 1991; Schunk, 1981). For example, self-efficacy and the various sources of self-efficacy (Usher & Pajares, 2006) are stronger predictors of mathematics achievement than general mental ability (Stevens, Olivárez, & Hamman, 2006). Once again, the "I can" attitude prevails. This reinforces the importance of a growth mindset in that it shows that attitudes play a key role in student motivation and performance.

Although a growth mindset based on the importance of effort should increase students' confidence to perform tasks, Schunk (1984) found that successful students who received feedback that complimented their ability rather than their effort developed higher self-efficacy and learning. Schunk (1984) suggested that teachers encourage students to use effort as an explanation for failure and to use ability as an explanation for success. On the surface this appears contradictory with self-theory research, which documents that recognition of effort promotes a growth mindset and subsequently improves student motivation and achievement. Dweck found that ability praise made participants' confidence and motivation fragile when they encountered difficulty (Grant & Dweck, 2003; Mueller & Dweck, 1998). It appears that ability praise works when students find their tasks easy but becomes problematic when they encounter difficulties. Because many gifted students are not being academically challenged, and their schoolwork requires little effort, effort praise might also not work for them if they did not expend any effort to be successful.

Recognizing Ability and Effort

My colleagues and I (Siegle, Rubenstein, Pollard, & Romey, 2010) have suggested that gifted students may be able to appreciate the role ability plays in achievement without necessarily developing a fixed entity view of talent development. We believe that high-achieving students might be able to appreciate their high ability without being paralyzed by an entity view. We found gifted students' beliefs about the role ability played in their performance varied with the self-perceived task. The gifted participants in one of our studies, who were identified for their high academic performance, saw ability as a stronger factor in nonacademic tasks such as dance than in academic tasks such as mathematics. Because all of the students in our study had been identified for their high academic achievement and not other talents such as music or art, we postulated that students may be more likely to believe effort is a factor in areas where they succeed (such as academics) and may believe ability is more of a factor in areas where they are not known for high achievement (such as music and art in this study). In this work, we also found that students' *interest in a topic* was a better predictor of self-perceived task performance than either their mindset or their perceptions of the importance of effort or ability. I discuss the importance of using students' interest in reversing underachievement in Chapter 9.

The key is to distinguish between recognition of talent and recognition of how the talent came to fruition, with the latter being crucial. Obviously, the attitude of parents and teachers is important. As Murphy and Dweck's (2010) work showed, the system in which individuals function influences how they self-display their mindset. Therefore, discussions with students should encompass the growth the students have made that brought their outstanding skills to be recognized. This discussion can be enhanced by sharing recently mastered work that had initially challenged the students.

Parents and teachers with foresight can keep samples of previous academic work and periodically review students' earlier work with the individual students to show growth and improvement. Students are often amazed at how easy their earlier work now appears and how much better they are now able to perform. Student portfolios also promote this sort of self-reflection. Students should help select work to include in their portfolios for future review (Siegle & McCoach, 2005b). These reviews not only enhance students' self-efficacy, they also have the potential to promote a growth mindset. They acknowledge the good work students are doing while drawing attention to the evolution that occurred on the path to reaching their high levels of performance. I will expand on these in Chapter 8.

Increasing Self-Efficacy
and Promoting Effort

In addition to the strategies that have already been shared, the ways parents and educators compliment students also have an impact on how successful students perceive themselves to be. Everyone agrees that students should be encouraged to work hard, as effort plays a significant role in achievement of challenging tasks. However, students also need to believe they have the skills to succeed. The key in complimenting students is once again to help them recognize that skills are developed, and that they have acquired or are in the process of acquiring the skills necessary to succeed. The feedback should contain (a) recognition of the skill and (b) attribution of its development to the student. By complimenting students on the specific skills they have developed, educators and parents can draw attention to each skill and to its development. This acknowledges the effort without drawing undue attention to it. An example is, "You did very well on this math project. You've learned how to solve equations." A statement such as "You are so smart" is counterproductive. It implies that abilities and skills are set and also does not help the student recognize what he or she is doing well.

Specific, rather than general, compliments are more effective. A general compliment such as, "Good work" doesn't carry the weight of something more specific such as, "You have really developed your skills at solving quadratic equations." Specific feedback provides students with an opportunity to appraise their progress by communicating two key pieces of information: what specific skill students possess and the recognition that they developed that skill. Both components may be necessary when working with students with an entity mindset because it recognizes the skills they have come to value while moving them toward appreciating the developmental nature of the skill. Students will reflect on the comment and think, "Yes, I have learned to solve quadratic equations."

Of course, compliments must be genuine and earned. Complimenting children for tasks they did not perform well or for unchallenging tasks can be counterproductive and diminish their trust. Overly effusive and too numerous compliments can backfire. The goal should be to help students recognize their developed skills and the effort put into them, not to heap undue praise.

As stated earlier, gifted students may develop a fixed mindset, which may limit their willingness to take academic risks. Gifted students who perceive their giftedness as innate may believe they had very little to do with their demonstrated abilities. Although it is true that gifted students often acquire skills more quickly and easily than their peers, they still gain such skills through learning. They may have taught themselves to read or learned to read easily at an early age, but they still learned to read. It is important for gifted students to recognize that the talents they possess are acquired, and they are capable of further developing these talents. As previously stated, reviewing earlier work can further this understanding.

Educators can also encourage students to compete with themselves by charting their earlier progress. Many children may remember a special spot in their home that their parents reserved to mark their height each year. The children loved to observe how much they grew. Just as parents chart height, educators can also help children recognize other forms of growth and development. Teachers can record a running list of mastered multiplication facts or geometric theorems or of particularly difficult problems students have solved.

Gifted students also need to understand that just because they find something difficult it does not mean they are not smart. As I will discuss in Chapter 5 (on perfectionism), not trying preserves an image for some students. They do not perceive "not trying" as poor performance. They can always say, "It wasn't important" or "I just rushed through it and didn't do my best." Young people often believe that if they need to work hard at school then they are not smart. In fact, peers often perceive hard-working students as less intelligent than students who do well in school without making any visible effort. Educators and parents can share stories of how experts and elite performers used deliberate practice (Ericsson, Krampe, & Tesch-Römer, 1993) to push the limits of their current abilities and systematically address their weaknesses.

The mantra needs to be, "Working hard makes us smarter." The key is to acknowledge ability while recognizing that effort went into its development.

A mindset intervention Dweck has used involves teaching students how the brain works and discussing its elasticity and potential for growth. This will also help students recognize that challenging tasks, such as those in an advanced mathematics class, help them become smarter.

Generic Versus Domain-Specific Giftedness

How gifts manifest themselves is another issue that can be discussed with students. Almost three decades have passed since Howard Gardner (1985) first introduced his Theory of Multiple Intelligences. Gardner's theory extended Calvin Taylor's (1986) earlier Multiple Talents work and illustrates there are many ways to be smart. Different domains of talent become more important as young people transition from childhood to adulthood. As Subotnik et al. (2011) noted, "Although general ability and potential may be the hallmarks of academic giftedness in children, domain-specific ability and achievement become increasingly important as individuals develop and increase their knowledge base in a field" (p. 39). When students are identified by high IQ scores, they probably demonstrate high levels of analytic functionality and the skills necessary to grapple with complexity (Kehle & Bray, 2011). Everyone has patterns of strengths and weaknesses, and interests also play into how involved individuals become in different areas (Siegle, Rubenstein, Pollard, et al., 2010).

It is rare for individuals to perform at outstanding levels in more than one domain. Although educators of the gifted often discuss multipotentiality among the gifted, Achter, Lubinski, and Benbow (1996) suggested that individuals rarely perform at extremely high levels across several different domains. As they stated, "gifted individuals may gain a better understanding of themselves (and each other) through a more refined appreciation of the unique and salient features of their individuality" (p. 73). For example, all students should be encouraged to challenge themselves and become better at mathematics, but it is also unrealistic to expect that every student, even those who had been identified as gifted with a high IQ, will excel at the highest levels of mathematics.

Educators and parents can share Gardner's (1985) work on the many ways to be smart. They can also remind students that being gifted doesn't just happen to someone: that the students themselves have something to do with developing their giftedness. Students can appreciate individual learning differences while recognizing that everyone has the potential to become smarter than they are now. In some sense, giftedness is lost when students fail to embrace talent development. As most in the field do, we call these individuals gifted underachievers. As Dai (2010) noted in his book on the nature and nurture of giftedness,

> Early manifestations of giftedness do not guarantee later success, as task environments at a higher level impose new demands and constraints. As a result, some stand out while others fade away. . . . Being gifted has different meanings at different stages of talent development. (p. 22)

Educators and parents can address students' developed mindsets in order to recognize the outstanding contributions young people are making without sabotaging, or possibly paralyzing, gifted students' future achievement. The key is to separate the recognition of the talent from the attribution for how the talent came to fruition.

"Talent development is a two-step process. First, we must provide opportunities for talent to surface, and then we must recognize that talent and help to move it to exceptional levels" (Siegle, 2008, p. 112). Highly developed skills must be recognized in order for educators and parents to provide educational opportunities that advance high-performing students to the even higher levels of excellence necessary for outstanding achievement. At the same time, students must recognize that it is their deliberate practice that moves their talent to the next level.

chapter 5

Addressing Issues of Perfectionism

Use what talents you possess; the woods would be very silent if no birds sang except those that sang best.

—Henry van Dyke

People who have a compulsive need to be in control of themselves, others, and life's risks often manifest this need in unhealthy perfectionism (Mallinger & DeWyze, 1992). They set unrealistic goals and then feel extremely frustrated when they or others cannot reach these goals (Greenspon, 2002). They spend an inordinate amount of time worrying about making mistakes (Adderholdt & Goldberg, 1999) in their desire to be perfect. Additionally, they fear being imperfect and may believe their acceptance as a person depends on their ability to be perfect (Greenspon, 2006). These unhealthy behaviors can ultimately contribute to underachievement. Perfectionism also provides the gifted child with an excuse for not performing. "Because perfectionism is unachievable, it provides the child with ready excuses for poor performance" (Davis, Rimm, & Siegle, 2011, p. 297).

Canadian psychologists Paul Hewitt and Gordon Flett (1991) identified three types of perfectionists: self-oriented, socially prescribed, and other-oriented. Self-oriented perfectionists set unrealistically high expectations on themselves. They set goals for themselves that are difficult, if not impossible, to obtain, and they have trouble accepting their own mistakes and shortcomings. Unlike the self-oriented perfectionist, socially prescribed perfectionists believe others are imposing perfection expectations on them. They worry about disappointing others when they fail to live up to the high standards that they perceive are expected of them, and they may resent the people whom they believe set these high expectations for them. The other-oriented perfectionists hold unrealistic expectations of others. These individuals have trouble delegating tasks, because they fear others will fail to perform tasks at the high standards they expect. They may redo work they have asked another to do and then resent the other person for having to redo the work (Antony & Swinson, 1998). Greenspon (2012) has suggested these types of perfectionism interact with each other, and it can be difficult to determine which type, or combination of types, represents the perfectionist behavior.

Common Behaviors of Perfectionists

Perfectionism is widespread. Some have estimated that about half the population has perfectionism tendencies (Adderholdt & Goldberg, 1999), although all of them are not unhealthy perfectionists. Even though there is not universal agreement (Greenspon, Parker, & Schuler, 2000), perfectionism is often seen as something that is multidimensional and can either be positive or negative. In other words, students can be perfectionists in different areas and their perfectionism can be unhealthy, which prevents them from pursuing new or challenging tasks, or it can be healthy, which allows them to be pursuers of excellence. Frost, Marten, Lahart, and Rosenblate (1990) have suggested perfectionism falls along six dimensions: order and organization, personal standards, concern over mistakes, parental expectations, parental criticism, and doubts about actions. Those who adhere to the healthy and unhealthy perfectionism theory see these dimensions as differing between adaptive and maladaptive perfectionism. A healthy perfectionist might set high personal standards, but not show excessive concern over mistakes, while an unhealthy perfectionist may be paralyzed by concern over mistakes, parental criticism, and doubts about actions. Dixon, Lapsley, and Hanchon (2004) noted that high scores on three of the maladaptive dimensions of perfectionism (concern over mistakes, parental criticism, and doubts about actions) seem to trump whatever advantages high scores on the adaptive dimension might otherwise convey. The absence of perfectionist tendencies is generally compatible with positive mental health, but some features of perfectionism, such as high organization and high personal standards (and parental expectations), could be cultivated to promote academic and personal adjustment.

For the purpose of this chapter, when I refer to perfectionism, I am referring to unhealthy perfectionists. I refer to healthy perfectionists as pursuers of excellence. Family therapist and psychologist Thomas Greenspon (2012) suggested the dividing line between perfectionists and pursuers of excellence is that although everyone is disappointed by failure, perfectionists are devastated by it. Unlike some researchers and practitioners in the field (Parker & Mills, 1996; Schuler, 2000), Greenspon does not believe it is possible to be a healthy perfectionist. He noted that "perfectionists may indeed be successful; this is despite their perfectionism, though, not because of it. It is not perfectionism that determines success; it is talent, energy, and commitment—all of which would likely remain if one's perfectionism somehow vanished" (Greenspon, 2012, p. 601).

Perfectionists often exhibit a set of reaction patterns that include:
- fear of failure,
- procrastination,
- dichotomous thinking,
- concentration on external rewards,
- workaholic tendencies,
- worry about the future,
- minimizing accomplishments, and
- a focus on mistakes (Adderholdt & Goldberg, 1999; Adderholdt-Elliot, 1987; Adelson & Wilson, 2009).

Fear of Failure

Perfectionism is about worrying about not being perfect. Perfectionists' performances are tied to their self-worth, so failure and mistakes bring into question their worth as a person. As long as they continue to excel, they can feel good about themselves. Perfectionists are crushed by negative comments. They are keenly more aware of the negative comments than the positive comments they receive.

Procrastination

Many unhealthy perfectionists procrastinate. Putting things off is their way to avoid the judgment they fear (Greenspon, 2006). This can be accomplished in two ways. They can simply procrastinate until they miss a deadline and thus produce nothing. Simply dropping out and "not playing" is one remedy for the anxiety these students are experiencing. Unfortunately, not participating can lead to underachievement by default.

An alternative pattern is to procrastinate until they are very near the deadline and then quickly pull something together. If the final product fails to meet their or others' expectations, they can blame their last-minute attempt and state they did not have sufficient time to "do a good job." Procrastination provides a perfect excuse. Not all procrastination is tied to perfectionism or underachievement. As a life-long procrastinator, I find that I work better under pressure. I simply cannot bring closure to what I hope to do until I am near the deadline. As the deadline approaches, my ideas flow, and I experience a productive rush. My wife, on the other hand, becomes paralyzed if a deadline is too close. Needless to say, working on projects together can be interesting. Although procrastination may or may not be a problem for procrastinators, it can be a problem for those who are working with them who function differently or who need the procrastinators' contribution before being able to complete their contribution to a project.

Dichotomous Thinking

When activities are progressing perfectly, perfectionists are on top of the world. However, as soon as events fail to unfold as expected, their attitudes dive. Life is a roller-coaster ride of perceived successes and failures where outcomes are viewed as either great or terrible with little middle ground. This dichotomous thinking may resemble that of someone who is manic-depressive.

Concentration on External Rewards

Although everyone enjoys being rewarded for good work, external rewards can be addictive for perfectionists. For some, a simple reward is not sufficient. Some perfectionists play a numbers game and expect to excel at everything. Instead of enjoying a top prize at the National History Day contest, they are disappointed because they did not also win the science fair. Nothing is good enough, and no number of awards is sufficient.

Workaholic Tendencies

Maintaining a balanced life is important. Even young people can become addicted to work. Just as it is important to work, it is also important to play. Adderholdt and Goldberg (1999) noted that workaholics burn out more often than those with a balanced life. Workaholics also suffer from higher stress levels. Both of these conditions lead to lower productivity.

Worry About the Future

Perfectionists may also fail to appreciate their current accomplishments because they are concerned about what lies ahead for them. Unhealthy perfectionists might do well on one test, but fail to celebrate because they are dreading next month's test. Their lives are in a constant state of anxiety as they await future failures.

Minimizing Accomplishments

Perfectionists can minimize their own accomplishments while exaggerating the accomplishments of others. In some cases, these students are attempting to compete with an imaginary composite that consists of the best traits of each of their friends. They might include the intelligence of one friend, academic ability of another, popularity of a third, and perhaps the physical appearance of a fourth. They fail to realize the image they are setting for themselves does not exist.

A Focus on Mistakes

Some perfectionists continually reflect on past performances that did not live up to their high expectations. These individuals are unable to move past these self-perceived failures. Consequently, they do not embrace new or challenging opportunities that will contribute to their continued growth and achievement. They obsess on missed opportunities or what they should have done rather than focus on what they can do to improve. Other perfectionists may believe what they are doing is not good enough and continually redo it. I have known students who completed assignments and then refused to submit them because they did not feel they were good enough. "Good enough" meant perfect.

At the heart of all of these behaviors is the issue of the perfectionist's self-esteem. Some of the above actions tend to lower self-esteem, while perfectionists use others to protect or bolster their self-esteem.

Perfectionism and Giftedness

Gifted students, like all students, can suffer from perfectionism. The research data do not suggest that gifted students are any more likely to suffer from perfectionism than other students (Adelson & Wilson, 2009; Dixon et al., 2004; Parker & Mills, 1996). However, when children's self-worth is tied to their giftedness and the high performance associated with it, then perfectionism is more likely to be an issue. Schuler (2000) has suggested that

> For a minority of gifted adolescents, perfectionism is a destructive force with detrimental consequences, while for most it is a healthy aspect of their lives resulting in positive growth. . . . Gifted adolescents need assistance in understanding that wanting to achieve at a high level, having a drive to excel, and enjoying order and organization are positive aspects of their perfectionism. (p. 194)

Of course, Schuler was discussing what she refers to as healthy perfectionism or a healthy pursuit of excellence. For those for whom perfectionism is destructive, it can result in high anxiety that interferes with their performance and can lead to their underachievement.

Contributing Factors to Perfectionism

Idea-Skill Gap

One reason gifted students may exhibit perfectionist characteristics is the "idea-skill gap" (Rivero, 2010). A gap often exists between the grand ideas that gifted students envision and the skills they possess to implement those ideas. This is particularly relevant for younger students. As a teacher of the gifted, I occasionally supervised students who were interested in making movies. The movies students were able to complete usually fell short of the movie productions they envisioned. They simply did not have the skills or the equipment to achieve what they imagined. Their disappointment in their final product often darkened what many times was an enjoyable—and could have been a fulfilling—learning experience.

Lack of Early Challenge

Some research (Speirs Neumeister, Williams, & Cross, 2009) has suggested that lack of challenge during gifted students' early academic experiences figures into perfectionism tendencies. Young students who experience lack of challenge and early academic success may come to expect perfection as the norm. Some of these students may also come to believe they are valued for the perfection they are producing, rather than for who they are as individuals. They may continue to be productive; however, the unhealthy belief they have developed about their importance is problematic. When these students finally are challenged academically, some will "step up to the plate" and embrace the challenge, while others will simply avoid performing in order to save face—not trying means not failing in their eyes. Other students who are unchallenged address their boredom by creating challenges for themselves by striving for perfection (Speirs Neumeister et al., 2009). As long as this remains a pursuit of excellence, the student usually does well. However, such a pattern can turn into unhealthy perfectionism, which is why some researchers (Greenspon, 2002) caution that any type of perfectionism is dangerous.

Birth Order

Birth order may also be a factor. Although some have suggested that firstborn students are more often perfectionists (Adderholdt & Goldberg, 1999), it may be sibling order that influences personality (Birth Order Plus, n.d.). One of the problems with research on birth order is the inability of researchers to compensate for family size. Nevertheless, parents tend to value and reward milestones their first child reaches. Such an environment can contribute to young children believing they are valued for their advanced performances.

Personality

Personality is also a contributing factor. Speirs Neumeister (2010) noted that the self-oriented perfectionists she has worked with indicated their perfectionism came from within themselves, rather than from some external source; however, personal characteristics can be shaped by external factors.

Parenting

Parenting style may also be a factor. Several studies (Rice, Ashby, & Preusser, 1996; Speirs Neumeister, 2004) have indicated that perfectionism is associated with an authoritarian parenting style. This is particularly true for socially prescribed perfectionists; however, this relationship may be mediated by attachment issues (Speirs Neumeister & Finch, 2006). "Secure individuals may be less likely than any of the other attachment styles to adopt perfectionistic tendencies, since they have a positive view of both themselves and others and do not place their self-worth contingent upon their achievement" (Speirs Neumeister & Finch, 2006, p. 240).

Children whose parents are perfectionists tend to also be perfectionists. Adderholdt-Elliot (1987) used the term "generational inheritance" to describe the passing of perfectionism from one generation to another. The connection could be genetic or environmental. For example, the social learning that occurs as children observe their parents modeling perfectionist tendencies may ultimately result in their offspring internalizing those behaviors.

Perfectionism has also been associated with dysfunctional families and substance abuse. Young people may believe that if they are perfect those in their lives with issues will be better able to control those issues.

Popular Culture

Popular culture is also a key factor. Young people are bombarded with advertisements that suggest they will be more popular and have more fun if they purchase a certain product. Celebrities promote an image of perfectionism. Retouch artists remove blemishes from celebrities' portraits and pounds from their waistlines. Less than perfect performances are rerecorded and edited to perfection. The media and advertisers tell young people that perfectionism is possible and certain lifestyles and products will make them happier.

Possible Solutions

A key issue for most perfectionists is their belief that they are valued for what they produce, rather than for who they are. Being identified as gifted and talented certainly puts gifted students at risk of developing this belief as well. Therefore, teachers and parents must be careful how they discuss giftedness and talent development with young people. Chapters 4 and 8 are devoted to this issue. Needless to say, our comments to gifted students can positively or negatively impact their perceptions of themselves and talents they possess.

Greenspon's Process for Acceptance

Greenspon (2012) proposed a four-step process for creating an environment of acceptance that helps individuals address their perfectionism through self-appreciation: empathy, encouragement, self-reflection, and dialogue. The first step involves empathy. During this phase, the counselor and student work together to understand the motivational forces behind the perfectionism. Through this process students may begin to feel better understood and worth listening to. In other words, the process of being valued beyond what one produces begins. The encouragement phase is about pointing out things about students that the counselor appreciates. These compliments need to be meaningful and authentic, and involve personal qualities, rather than performances. Some self-examination may be necessary here. My own experience has shown that individuals who have trouble receiving compliments generally also have trouble giving genuine ones to others. The third phase of self-reflection involves helping students develop a deeper understanding of what mistakes mean to them and how they perceive that others view them. The final dialogue phases involve talking together about what mistakes mean, what people's expectations are, and why being less than perfect is frightening.

Through this dialogue, bonds that create a sense of acceptance are solidified and possible avenues for change are discovered.

Although most researchers agree that how students view their worth lies at the crux of the perfectionism issue, researchers (Adderholdt-Elliott, 1987; Adelson & Wilson, 2009; Speirs Neumeister, 2010) have also proposed strategies to address some of the behaviors that perfectionists exhibit. I describe some of their suggestions below.

Debugging Mistakes

Adults in children's lives should model taking on challenges and should share with young people how mistakes are useful. This can include discussing how mistakes hold a key role in growing and learning. Adderholdt-Elliott (1987) suggested sharing the computer programmer's debugging strategy. The original code that computer programmers create is often filled with errors. Rather than discard the code and begin again, the programmer systematically "debugs" the program. This practice is a good lesson to share with young people. Mistakes are not a terminal end; they are fixable events on the path to success. As a teacher, I often observed students crumple and discard a piece of paper when they were attempting to write a story. Debugging teaches students not to discard work that they find unsatisfactory. The lesson is to view their unsatisfactory work as fixable and to go about debugging it and making it better.

Swiss Cheese

Perfectionists can be overwhelmed by large tasks. One strategy that works well is to break larger tasks into smaller pieces. A key roadblock for many people is starting a large project. Often, taking the first step is the most difficult part of the process (see Chapter 11). If larger tasks can be broken into smaller pieces, they seem more manageable. This works well for two reasons. First, once the student has been successful at the initial tasks, the larger task becomes less daunting. Second, after some progress has been made through the smaller steps, the student becomes invested in the project and will want to finish it.

Teachers can also provide students with multiple opportunities to do well on assignments. This decreases the tension that perfectionists feel to only submit work they believe is perfect.

Creative Visualization

New or unfamiliar tasks are particularly threatening to perfectionists and can often paralyze them. One successful strategy for addressing new or unfamiliar tasks is to visualize the event or task as being completed before one actually tackles it. Perhaps a student is anxious about participating in a local spelling bee. A teacher or parent can spend some time discussing the contest with the student. This could include describing the setting and where various individuals will be standing or sitting. This "walk through" can address any questions or fears a student has about the event. If the visualization is done well, students will become sufficiently familiar with the event so that when they actually participate, it will feel like a comfortable rerun.

Creative Outlets

Because perfectionism is tied to self-worth, it can be helpful for perfectionists to participate in activities that are noncompetitive or do not involve judgment. Perfectionists should participate in these activities for the pleasure of doing them. The competitive nature of an activity depends on how it is structured. For example, running can either be competitive or noncompetitive. When I was younger, I found running in the evening to be an excellent way to relax after a busy day. I ran alone using a number of different routes. My friends would invite me to join them in local races. As a recovering perfectionist, I thanked them for the offer, but declined. Running was a relaxing time for me. I did not wish to add the pressure of competing with others in a race or tracking my time to the experience. A perfectionist can turn any activity into a quest for perfection, so this strategy only works if perfectionists are willing to put their perfectionism aside and embrace activities for the simple pleasure they bring.

Bibliotherapy

Pehrsson and McMillen (2007) noted that "stories affect human emotions, and books can serve as models for development" (p. 1). The idea of using books as therapy has been around for at least a century; however, it has only recently become popular. Pehrsson and McMillen proposed the following guidelines when selecting books for bibliotherapy:

- ❧ Books should be thoroughly read before suggesting them for use.
- ❧ The book should be current, credible, and relevant to the issue for which it is being used (in our case, perfectionism).
- ❧ Books should embrace cultural respect and inclusiveness.
- ❧ The bibliotherapy process needs to be facilitated and should include follow up to determine its effectiveness.

Hynes and Hynes-Berry (1994) proposed that the bibliotherapy process unfolds through four stages: recognition, examination, juxtaposition, and self-application. The first stage involves catching students' attention with something they read. The second stage involves students reflecting on their personal feelings and responses to the issue in question. These stages are followed by a deeper level of understanding where students merge their current understanding of the issue with new feelings that may have emerged from the reading. Finally, students evaluate their perspectives and begin integrating them into their actions.

Hébert's (2011) text on social and emotional needs of gifted students and Adelson and Wilson's (2009) paperback on perfectionism both provided useful lists of books and movies that can be used for bibliotherapy with gifted students. One popular book for this purpose is Stephen Manes' 1982 classic, *Be a Perfect Person in Just Three Days!* The story features Milo Crinkley, who wants to be perfect and discovers a book in the library with steps, such as wearing broccoli around his neck, to achieve his goal. He soon learns being perfect is not all he thought it could be.

Our goal is to help students become pursuers of excellence instead of being trapped in a perfectionism cycle that actually prevents them from doing their best. Ultimately, all of us need to learn that mistakes are an essential part of the learning process. We also need to learn that if we wait for perfection, we will produce very little. The renowned photographer Ansel Adams has been quoted as saying, "the perfect is the enemy of the good." If he had waited for everything in the scene he was photographing to be exactly right, he might never have tripped the shutter and created the beautiful black and white photographs that the world has come to enjoy (Price, 2011). We must help young people understand that if they place too high a standard on themselves and others, they will restrict their options and miss a lifetime of opportunities.

chapter 6

Rimm's Trifocal Model

> *Change your thoughts and you change the world.*
>
> —Norman Vincent Peale

No book on underachievement of gifted students is complete without a thorough discussion of the contribution of psychologist Sylvia Rimm. Rimm has spent her career counseling gifted underachievers and reversing their underachievement. She is well known for her appearances on the *TODAY* show, her radio talk show, her syndicated newspaper columns, and her many books. Based on clinical work with underachievers at the Family Achievement Clinic, Rimm (2008) developed the Trifocal Model. The Trifocal Model, which has been successful in about 80% of the clinic cases that used it (Rimm, 2003), typically requires about 6 months to turn around underachievement (Rimm, 2008). The model's name is derived from the three-way focus placed on the student, the home, and the school. The key component is coordinated collaboration between family and school in reversing underachievement and helping students feel good about themselves. The underlying principle of the model is that underachievement behaviors are learned, and therefore they can be unlearned. In this chapter,

I review the six steps of the Trifocal Model. My own Achievement Orientation Model (see Chapters 7–11) theoretically aligns with the six steps of the Trifocal Model. Readers who are interested in learning more about Rimm's work will find a plethora of resources on her website at http://www.sylviarimm.com.

The six steps of the model are:

1. Assessment of Skills, Abilities, Reinforcement Contingencies, and Types of Underachievement
2. Communication
3. Changing the Expectations of Important Others
4. Role Model Identification
5. Correcting Skill Deficiencies
6. Modifications of Reinforcements at Home and School (Davis et al., 2011, p. 315).

Assessment of Skills, Abilities, Reinforcement Contingencies, and Types of Underachievement

The first step in addressing underachievement is conducting a comprehensive assessment of the student. This serves at least three purposes. First, the assessment documents what the student is actually capable of achieving; it eliminates possible roadblocks, such as a learning disability, that could be hampering the student's performance. Second, a comprehensive assessment can provide useful information about the student's learning styles, strengths, and weaknesses. This information is essential for meeting the student's learning needs and remediating deficits in basic skills that may have developed as a result of the underachievement. Finally, because different types of underachievers exhibit different behavior patterns, the assessment reveals and identifies the underlying behaviors the student exhibits.

A school psychologist or counselor can conduct the assessment. Rimm has suggested that whoever conducts the assessment should have some background in educational assessment, be aware of different learning styles and motivational patterns, and understand the educational characteristics of gifted and creative students (Davis et al., 2011). The testing usually involves an individual IQ test, individual achievement tests to assess student strengths and deficits in basic skills, creativity assessments, surveys, and parent and student interviews. The formal assessments (IQ, achievement, and creativity tests) are useful in measuring the extent of the problem and the direction of the underachieving behavior (Rimm, 2008). Rimm has also created a number of instruments for measuring the dimensions of underachievement (AIM, GAIM, and AIM-TO). These are useful in classifying the various behaviors underachievers exhibit.

Rimm (2008) has found that students tend to fall into one of four categories of underachievement based on the data collected in the assessment. These categories are dependent conformers, dependent non-conformers, dominant conformers, and dominate nonconformers. Rimm cautioned that each child is unique, and these generalizations should only be used to focus on main characteristics. Dependent children tend to "manipulate people in their environments covertly in ways that require more than the typical assistance and encouragement. Their words and body language reach out for more help than they should need" while dominant children "relate to adults in their environment in more overtly aggressive ways. Because they function comfortably only when they are dominating a situation, they feel out of control when they are not mastering their environment. They will argue and debate" (Rimm, 2008, p. 169). Dependent children display a "poor me" image while dominant children tend to continually challenge. "Conforming underachievers are less visible than nonconforming underachievers. They tend to mask their problems, which are less extreme" (Rimm, 2008, p. 170). Readers are advised to refer to *Why Bright Kids Get Poor Grades and What You Can Do About It* (Rimm, 2008) or *Underachievement Syndrome: Causes and Cures* (Rimm, 1986) for thorough descriptions of each of these classifications. Figure 3 shows each of the categories and some common behaviors associated with each.

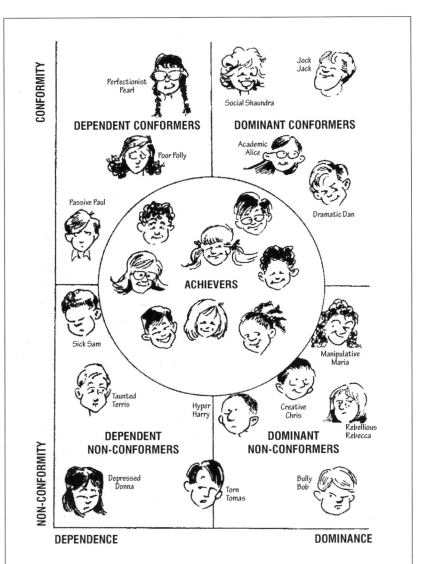

Figure 3. Sylvia Rimm's inner circle of achievers. Adapted from *Why Bright Kids Get Poor Grades and What You Can Do About It: A Six-Step Program for Parents and Teachers* (3rd ed., p. 10), by S. Rimm, 2008, Scottsdale, AZ: Great Potential Press. Copyright 2008 by Great Potential Press. Reprinted with permission of the author.

All of the information from the assessments is helpful when developing a plan to reverse the underachievement. This information is essential when communicating with others, and the student, about the student's potential. These communications are part of the second step in the Trifocal Model.

Communication

The assessment information is communicated to parents and teachers to help them understand the student's abilities and achievements as well as any dependence or dominance issue that may be reinforcing the underachievement. This discussion usually occurs via a parent-teacher conference. The goal of the conference is for all parties to understand what behaviors are taking place, to understand the motivation behind those behaviors, and to set mutual goals for the student. This involves setting realistic behavior and grade goals. Target grades should not be set unrealistically high; initial goals that are set too high can provide the student with an excuse for giving up. Short-term goals should be set slightly above where the student is currently achieving, but must be sufficiently challenging so that the student needs to "reach" to achieve them. Long-term expectations will be higher. When starting to reverse underachievement, the desired behavior is for the student to complete work on time with studying and effort. The discussion between parents and teachers should include what changes are being made at school and possible modifications parents plan to make at home. Whenever possible, both parents should attend the parent-teacher conference.

The communication component does not end with this conference. Communication between home and school needs to be a regularly planned activity as the student's progress is monitored. The direction of these progress reports should not be restricted to information sent from the school to the home. Parents can initiate communications and should be actively involved in sharing their perceptions about how well their student is progressing. The teacher also needs to apprise parents of the student's progress at completing assignments. These communications can be an e-mail or written note that reflects the percent of assignments completed, classroom effort being put forth, classroom behavior, and a list of any missing assignments. Rimm noted that the method of tracking progress between home and school must be foolproof. It cannot depend on the student, who will likely share good news only with each party and ignore or hide bad reports. Achievement requires accountability.

Rimm (2008) recommended parents should meet with primary-age students on a daily basis to discuss their progress. Similar meetings with upper elementary and secondary students can occur less frequently, possibly weekly. As progress is made, the frequency of the meetings is lowered.

Although the next three steps will be discussed separately, they actually occur concurrently.

Changing the Expectations of Important Others

The assessment data are also useful in changing the student's as well as others' expectations. In the case of the student, this may address self-efficacy issues that will be discussed in Chapter 8. For the teacher, it may encourage and influence instructional and curricular modifications that make school more meaningful for the student. I discuss increasing meaningfulness in Chapter 9. Additionally, students may now perceive that teachers want them to succeed. This communication also addresses parental expectations for the student. The students' changing perceptions of teacher and parent support and expectations are reflected in the student having a positive environmental perception. This is discussed in depth in Chapter 10.

Student

Students need to believe that they have the skills to do well, and that their achievement is attached to the effort they put forth. Although it may seem strange, many underachievers do not see the relationship between effort and productivity. They do not believe their effort will make a difference. In some sense, they are waiting for their talent to be discovered but apply no effort to develop their skills themselves. "The unrealistic belief that children will suddenly be recognized as extraordinary does little to give them hope and only exaggerates their sense of disappointment about their own poor performance" (Rimm, 2008, p. 203).

Some underachievers also set unrealistically high expectations and then wait for luck to manifest these expectations. Most often, underachievers are stuck in their pattern of underperformance brought on by limited effort on their part. This can be a difficult cycle to break. Students need to understand that success results from effort, not luck. I reviewed this issue in depth in Chapter 4.

The first step in breaking the underachievement cycle is helping students understand they have the ability to do well and that they possess the power to change their performance. This might involve sharing some of the assessment data from Step 1 with them. Most psychologists would not recommend sharing exact scores with students; however, sharing that a given score is well above average might be appropriate. At the same time, the student needs to commit to reaching some short-term, attainable goals. In other words, students need to understand they have the potential to improve their academic situation, but it will require effort and a change in their work habits. They also need to understand that this change involves real progress over time.

Parents and teachers should recognize the progress students are making toward their goals. Students will quickly become discouraged if no one acknowledges their successes, however small they may be. However, parents and teachers must avoid overly praising or making too much of a student's accomplishments. My sister, who had been an average student in high school, earned straight-A grades during her first semester of community college. Those around her were elated with her performance. She became quite anxious as a result of the high praise she received. She commented that she worried everyone would be expecting all-A grades from her all of the time. Extreme praise can be problematic, particularly with perfectionists (see Chapter 5). Rimm has suggested that parents and teachers avoid "*est*"-ness when describing student's accomplishments (Rimm, Siegle, & McCoach, 2011). Words like b*est*, great*est*, strong*est*, and smart*est* can be time bombs that can ultimately lead to nonproductive behavior. Perfectionists will be paralyzed by them. Dependent students may be intimidated by them. Dominant students may feel overly empowered by them.

The student, as well as parents and teachers, should understand that breaking the habits of the underachieving cycle takes effort and time. As Rimm (2008) noted, students "should realize that while working, they will sometimes feel stressed, impatient, and disappointed in themselves, but that all of these feelings are signs of motivation and a true index that they are on the correct route" (p. 202).

Home

I have already discussed the importance of recognizing students' progress, but not overly praising them for their accomplishments. Parents should share their reasonable expectations with their students. Parents need to be clear that they expect the student to put effort into his or her schoolwork, and they expect the work to be completed on time. This might include rules about completing homework immediately after school and before watching television, playing video games, or using the Internet for social purposes. Through this discussion, students and parents can reach an agreement on acceptable short- and long-term goals. Ultimately, the student needs to accept ownership of these goals, but the parents must remain vigilant in monitoring the student's progress, appropriately recognizing progress when it is made, and encouraging the student. This involves recognizing small efforts that will ultimately grow into patterns of achievement.

Parents also need to modify their own behavior. How parents view their daily work experiences is often reflected in how students view school. A comment such as, "I work hard all day, and I don't seem to accomplish anything" sends a message that effort and hard work do not pay off. More information on this is included in the modeling section later in this chapter.

Parents also need to encourage achievement in the home. The renowned educational psychologist Benjamin Bloom published a landmark study on talent development in 1985. He and his colleagues spent 4 years studying the teachers and families of 150 world-class pianists, Olympic swimmers, sculptors, tennis champions, research mathematicians, and research neurologists. Some key findings in the families of these eminent individuals included:

- Parents exhibited a strong work ethic. The significance of doing well was evident in the home and was applied to activities at home and school at an early age.
- An attitude of work before play prevailed in the home.
- Self-discipline was taught, and the children of the family were expected to help with household chores and to do them well.
- The parents were usually involved in the talent activity, and the student's interest and involvement in the activity were considered part of being a member of the family.
- Curiosity was encouraged in the home, and parents took time to answer questions and research answers when they didn't know them.

Naturally, parents must communicate a united front when working with the student. A dominating underachiever will quickly recognize parental conflict and may play the parents against each other to avoid tasks he or she finds undesirable. Changing home expectations may also involve changing the expectations of siblings. Rimm (1986) suggested the following procedure when communicating with siblings:

[Informing siblings] should be done privately so that each sibling is given support for the expected change in status and has been given a clear message by parents that any discouragement of their sibling, no matter how subtle, will not be tolerated. If this communication is given in private to achieving children, the message is more likely to be taken seriously. . . . [Achieving children] should view their sibling's achievements as something in which they can share, not as a "put down" to their own personal accomplishment. Teaching siblings to admire each other's performance is a valuable counterbalancing technique in dealing with difficult sibling rivalry. (pp. 177–178)

School

The classroom teacher must believe the student is capable of doing better. Test scores can provide convincing evidence. Generally, gifted and talented students who underachieve tend to show a decline in achievement over time. Documenting this decline provides additional evidence for teachers that something must be done now to reverse the cycle of declining achievement.

The student and teacher can discuss the higher expectations that both expect. Like parents, teachers need to recognize new efforts the student expends and the progress the student is making. Teachers should use specific rather than general comments when recognizing student progress. Rather than saying, "Good work on this paper," the teacher might say, "Your effort has paid off; you have written well-constructed sentences." Written comments on papers as well as private messages are more effective than comments in front of the class. The purpose of teacher feedback is threefold. First, it lets the student know that others are recognizing and appreciating the effort he or she is putting forth. Second, it helps the student realize that he or she does have the ability to do better. Finally, it suggests a connection between the student's effort and accomplishment. The importance of specific, developmental comments is discussed in more detail in Chapters 4 and 8.

The teacher must build a trusting relationship with the student. Through their partnership, the student and teacher come to understand that the student can and will do better.

Role-Model Identification

Step 4 involves the discovery of a role model. Hébert and Olenchak (2000) collaborated on three case studies of underachievers. They discovered that mentors dramatically influenced the underachieving males they studied. Hébert (2011) reported, "the overarching finding in this research was the powerful influence of a significant adult" (p. 262). Rimm concurred when she wrote, "All other treatments for underachievement dim in importance compared with strong identification with an achieving model" (Davis et al., 2011, p. 318). Many underachieving students do not have an achieving role model with whom they can relate. In these cases, one must be introduced into their lives. Possible role models include parents, relatives, coaches, teachers, tutors, mentors, older students, and youth group leaders. Effective role models are seen as similar to the student they are mentoring, are perceived by the student as nurturing to him or her, and are seen as having some power. In addition to these characteristics, Rimm has added openness and willingness to share their own real experiences, willingness to give time, and a sense of positive accomplishment to the list of characteristics for effective role models (Davis et al., 2011).

Parents can be outstanding role models. However, if a parent is not serving that role for some reason, a role model needs to be introduced into an underachiever's life. The purpose of the role model is to expose the student to someone who demonstrates that effort and hard work produce positive outcomes. This is someone who finds his or her work fulfilling. Students learn to imitate achievement-oriented behaviors when they have a respected other who models it for them. In my own case, such a role model entered my life 4 years after I graduated from high school when I began working at a small newspaper. The work ethic that Fred Roach, the owner of the newspaper, modeled is the reason I finally decided to attend college for the first time at age 26. It is probably the reason I ultimately earned a Ph.D. and wrote this book. Fred's role in my life in no way diminished the important roles that both of my parents held in my life; he simply modeled a work perspective that I had not previously encountered. After working side-by-side with him, I began adopting new organization skills and setting more challenging goals for myself.

Unfortunately, some students who underachieve never encounter such a model. Or, they may become attracted to an inappropriate model. Rimm (1986) noted:

> young adults who may not have established their own identities, and who may be confused about their own direction, may be readily available negative models for underachieving teenagers. Since they are older and appear more experienced, powerful and exciting, youths who see their own frustration as similar to those of flashy young adults are ready prey. (pp. 185–186)

Of course, the key to overcoming this problem is not to create a vacuum for this to occur. The key is being an appropriate model who recognizes the positive aspects in the student, shares satisfaction over work well done, and avoids a cycle of continually criticizing the student.

Correct Skill Deficiencies

Students with a pattern of underachievement usually have skill deficiencies as a result of inattention in class and poor work habits. Fortunately, because the students are gifted, these deficits can usually be quickly overcome with tutoring. Of course, the extent and length of the underachievement will determine how much work is needed to correct skill deficiencies.

Although one-on-one tutoring is probably most effective for this process, it comes with a price, and every effort should be made to avoid fostering dependence. Rimm warned:

> The correction of skill deficiencies must be conducted carefully so that (1) the independent work of the underachieving child is reinforced by the tutor, (2) manipulation of the tutor by the child is avoided, and (3) the child senses the relationship between effort and the achievement outcomes. Charting progress during tutoring helps visually confirm the rapid progress to both child and tutor. Breaking larger tasks into smaller tasks permits the students to build confidence. (Davis et al., 2011, p. 319)

Modifications of Reinforcements at Home and School

Finally, counselors, parents, and teachers can collaborate on making changes that support the student's achievement and discourage some of the behaviors that have fed the student's underachievement. These changes will include long-term goals and short-term objectives that guarantee immediate small successes for the student at home and school. These successful experiences can be reinforced by rewards that are small but meaningful to the student. I discuss the use of rewards in Chapter 9.

Home and school modifications extend far beyond considering a reward structure. Our work on underachievement (McCoach & Siegle, 2003a, 2003b) has shown that many gifted underachievers simply do not see school as meaningful. This may be because parents have failed to stress the importance of school to the student. It may be that the curriculum is too easy for the student, and the student should be accelerated or grade skipped to a higher grade. It may be that the student's interests are not being recognized and nurtured. It may be that the importance of school is not fully understood by the student. I discuss strategies for making school more meaningful in Chapter 9.

Throughout this chapter, the reader may feel that the fault of underachievement lies with the student. Although the focus has been on the student's behavior and how to modify it, the reasons for that behavior are varied. A number of factors contribute to student under-achievement (e.g., inappropriate school curriculum, no role model, underachieving peer group, oppositional parents). Each of these factors can contribute to students being caught in a cycle of being overly dependent or overly dominant. Such patterns drive behaviors and ultimately influence academic achievement. Each student who underachieves is different, but underachievers do share some common behavior patterns.

chapter 7

Achievement Orientation Model

Students' Beliefs That Regulate Their Motivation to Achieve

They can because they think they can.

—Virgil

Why do some students achieve while other, equally talented students do not? One possible reason is the attitudes they hold toward given tasks. Previous research on underachievement and motivation theory provides a clue to what attitudes may be important for achievement. On the basis of this previous work, D. Betsy McCoach and I developed the Achievement Orientation Model. This model (see Figure 4) is founded on Bandura's self-efficacy theory, Weiner's attribution theory, Eccles' expectancy-value theory, and Lewin's person-environment fit theory. The model suggests that individuals' self-perceptions in three areas (self-efficacy, goal valuation [meaningfulness], and environmental perception) regulate students' motivation, and subsequently, their academic achievement. Accordingly, individuals must possess a positive attitude within each of the three areas. The intensity of their attitude in the three areas need not be equally strong, but it must be positive. The three attitudes direct a resultant behavior (self-regulation) that supports achievement. According to the model,

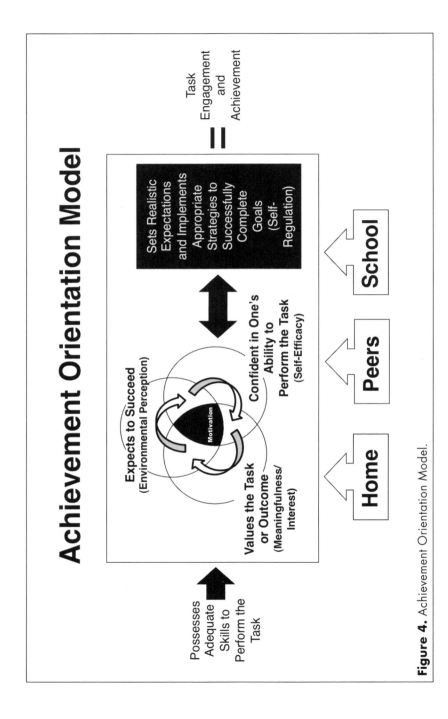

Figure 4. Achievement Orientation Model.

if any one of the three components is low, regardless of the strength of the others, motivation is affected. The three components of the Achievement Orientation Model will be discussed in further detail in the following sections.

Self-Efficacy

Students must believe they have the skills to do well before they will tackle a task. As previously noted, Albert Bandura first coined the term self-efficacy for this trait in the late 1970s. Self-efficacy, one of the most consistently defined motivational constructs (Murphy & Alexander, 2001), refers to individuals' judgments about being able to perform a particular activity. It is an individual's "I can" or "I can't" belief. Research over the past 30 years has revealed a positive relationship between self-efficacy beliefs and academic performance and persistence (Multon et al., 1991). The relationship exists across a wide variety of subjects, experimental designs, and assessment methods. Those with high self-efficacy are not only more likely to attempt tasks, but they also work harder and persist longer in the face of difficulties (Bandura, 1986; Lyman et al., 1984; Schunk, 1981). When students don't believe they have the skills to do well in a subject, they will not attempt it.

Self-efficacy judgments are based on four sources of information: an individual's own past performance, vicarious experiences of observing the performances of others, verbal persuasion that one possesses certain capabilities, and physiological states (Bandura, 1986). These four sources have been found to influence both academic and self-regulation efficacy beliefs (Usher & Pajares, 2006).

However, students should not only believe they have the skills to do well in a subject, they should believe the skills they have are malleable and can be further improved and developed through effort (Dweck & Molden, 2005). Generally, gifted students have high academic self-efficacy and do not attribute their academic failures to lack of ability (Assouline, Colangelo, Ihrig, & Forstadt, 2006; Chan,

1996). Their issue may be, "To what do they attribute their ability?" Although it is imperative that children recognize their skills and understand that they can do well if they attempt tasks, it is important that they also recognize their own role in developing their talents. As noted in Chapter 4, Dweck (1999) has found that individuals who believe their abilities have been developed and are not fixed by some innate force are more likely to attempt challenging tasks. Gifted students are especially at risk of believing their abilities are innate and not developed, particularly if others in their lives have not discussed their giftedness with them. Therefore, it is imperative that gifted students are not only efficacious about their capacity to perform well, but also understand the important role that effort plays in developing abilities.

Task Meaningfulness

Students must also find school tasks meaningful and valuable. Even if students believe they have the skills (self-efficacy) to do well in school, if they do not see their schoolwork as meaningful, they will not complete it. Many gifted students do not see the work they are doing in school as meaningful for several reasons. They may already know much of what is being presented to them (Reis et al., 1993). Generally, gifted students are able to process information faster and at a much higher level than other students (Davis et al., 2011). They may also find the work they are given is not intellectually stimulating (McCoach & Siegle, 1999). They also often have specific passion areas they enjoy exploring (Renzulli & Reis, 1997), but are seldom given opportunities to pursue their interests in school. Traditional school settings, as compared to gifted and advanced classes, often undermine rather than support academic passion (Fredricks, Alfeld, & Eccles, 2010) by failing to take these factors into account. In a recent study (Garn et al., 2010), a majority of parents of gifted students saw the motivational climate at school as contributing to motivation issues they faced with their children. These parents saw classroom practices such as lack of challenge and meaning in school assignments as barriers to their children's academic motivation.

Generally speaking, gifted students enjoy learning and do not want to be bored in school. However, they often equate lack of challenge with boredom (Gallagher, Harradine, & Coleman, 1997). Baum et al. (1995) reversed underachievement when they provided opportunities for students to explore personal interests and create authentic products and services by working on projects in a manner similar to practicing professionals (Renzulli & Reis, 1997). Fredricks et al. (2010) recommended similar activities for gifted students based on their work.

Wigfield and Eccles (2000) have devoted considerable effort to examining goal valuation; they developed the expectancy-value theory. This theory describes student motivation as a product of a student's valuation of a task and expectations of success. With respect to task valuation, Wigfield and Eccles proposed that students are motivated by a task associated with high attainment value (i.e., the importance of doing well on a specific task), high intrinsic value (i.e., the enjoyment individuals receive when completing a task), high utility value (i.e., the usefulness of the task for future goals), and a moderately low cost (i.e., what the individual will have to give up to succeed with or engage in a task). The expectations for the success component fall under the perception of the environmental component of the Achievement Orientation Model. I discuss this component in the next section.

Perceptions of the Environment

Students' perceptions of school and home events, the nature of teachers' and parents' expectations and support, and the patterns of interaction between students, teachers, and parents have an impact on their academic attitudes and behaviors. The way students look at situations, places, and things reflects the way they view the world and influences the conclusions and decisions they make (Greene, 2001).

For example, a student may perceive that a particular classroom environment is not a safe place to voice her opinions or make mistakes. This perception may prove to be totally accurate. If this is the case, then the student can be helped to learn how to deal better with this situation, and the teacher may be willing to make some changes in either his interactions with the student or in the physical classroom environment. If, however, the perception that the classroom is not a safe place is unfounded, then the student can learn the necessary skills to do the cognitive work required to change the inaccurate perception. It is important that students do not fall victim to external forces. There are situations and aspects of situations that they can control, provided they have the skills to determine this (Greene, 2001).

Although some environmental factors are within an individual's control, others are not. Ogbu (1978) noted that people put their effort into areas where they believe they can be successful and in environments where they believe they are supported. For example, Worrell (2007) noted that the relationship between ethnic identity exploration/affirmation and academic achievement was moderated by the environment for African American students. Thus, perceptions of the environment factor significantly in achievement motivation.

Students must believe that those around them value them and want to see them succeed. Their perceptions of their environment can spur them to work hard or can dishearten them. Some students believe the "deck is stacked against them," and that any effort they put forth will be thwarted. Students who view their environment as friendly and reinforcing may be more likely to demonstrate motivated behavior. A phrase such as, "My teachers does not understand me" may be a sign that students do not view their environment as friendly, or that they have developed a belief that their efforts do not affect outcomes (Rathvon, 1996). These students may believe they have the ability to perform well on a particular school topic, and they may even believe that the topic is important to learn; however, if they do not believe that their attempt at the task will be successful (for whatever reason), they will not engage or be productive.

Engagement and Self-Regulation

Students who have positive attitudes in the three areas of self-efficacy, task meaningfulness, and environmental perceptions set realistic goals and self-regulate. If any one of these three attitudes is low, individuals can fail to engage and achieve. Self-regulation and study skills are important for academic success. However, they are a resultant behavior of positive attitudes that enable students to be successful, rather than a driving force associated with underachievement among gifted students. My experience working with gifted students has shown that making school more meaningful appears to be the most effective strategy to address student underachievement. Many gifted students have the skills to be successful; they simply are not choosing to engage and apply those skills because they do not see the meaningfulness in the tasks they are being asked to do. For most underachievers, teaching them study skills does little to improve their academic achievement. For many gifted underachievers, self-regulation is a byproduct of the interaction of the self-efficacy, task meaningfulness, and environmental perceptions beliefs. In the Achievement Orientation Model, we posit that self-regulation is a byproduct of being efficacious about a task, believing the task is valuable, and trusting that the environment and those in it support achievement.

chapter 8

Self-Efficacy

Increasing Students' Confidence to Learn

> *Puff, puff, chug, chug, went the Little Blue Engine. "I think I can – I think I can – I think I can. . . ." "Hurray, hurray," cried the funny little clown and all the dolls and toys. . . . And the Little Blue Engine smiled.*
>
> —Watty Piper

Some students are confident about their ability to tackle new or challenging tasks. Other students are not. What makes one student believe in his ability while another doubts his skills? Researchers over the past 30 years have successfully examined this issue and have developed a variety of easy-to-implement strategies that will increase students' confidence to learn new material (Siegle & McCoach, 2007). Although no single strategy works with all students, a combination of these techniques can increase your students' confidence in their ability to achieve. This confidence is referred to as self-efficacy (Bandura, 1977).

What Is Self-Efficacy, and Why Is It Important?

As stated in Chapter 4, self-efficacy is a person's judgment about being able to perform a particular activity. It is a student's "I can" or "I cannot" belief. Unlike self-esteem, which reflects how students feel about their worth or value, self-efficacy reflects how confident students are about performing specific tasks. High self-efficacy in one area may not coincide with high self-efficacy in another area. Just as high confidence in playing football may not be matched with high confidence in playing baseball, high self-efficacy in mathematics does not necessarily accompany high self-efficacy in spelling. Self-efficacy is specific to the task being attempted. For example, a student may be very efficacious about her algebra skills, but not so efficacious about her geometry skills.

Unfortunately, having high self-efficacy does not guarantee that students believe they will be successful. Self-efficacy refers to beliefs about behaviors, not consequences (Owen, 1989). Regardless of one's efficacy expectations, outcomes may vary because individuals are not motivated to behave in ways that they believe lead to negative results, nor are they motivated toward outcomes that they do not value (Schunk, 1989b). Although self-efficacy indicates how strongly students believe they have the skills to do well, they may believe other factors will keep them from succeeding. These other factors include how valuable they see the task, how much effort they believe will be required to complete the task, and what type of support (or roadblock) they find in the environment. I discuss these in Chapters 9 and 10.

Although having a strong self-efficacy is not sufficient for students to be motivated to tackle tasks, it is a necessary component. A growing body of research reveals that there is a positive, significant relationship between students' self-efficacy beliefs and their academic performance (Bandura, 1993; Collins, 1984; Multon et al., 1991). People with low self-efficacy toward a task are more likely to avoid it, while those with high self-efficacy are not only more likely to attempt the task, but will also work harder and persist longer in the face of difficulties (Ames, 1990; Bandura, 1977, 1986; Schunk, 1981). Self-efficacy influences (a) what activities students select, (b) how much effort they put forth, (c) how persistent they are in the face of difficulties, and (d) the difficulty of the goals they set. Students with low self-efficacy do not expect to do well, and they often do not achieve at a level that is commensurate with their abilities. Because they do not believe they have the skills to do well, they often will not try.

The connection between self-efficacy and achievement grows stronger as students advance through school. By the time students are in college, their self-efficacy beliefs are more strongly related to their achievement than any measure of their ability (Wood & Locke, 1987). If we wish to develop high educational achievement among our students, it is essential that we begin building stronger self-efficacy as early as possible. My goal with this chapter is to describe factors that influence students' self-efficacy and to provide some strategies that have been shown to increase the self-efficacy of students who lack confidence in their ability to succeed.

As noted in Chapters 4 and 7, in addition to students having high self-efficacy and believing they have the necessary skills to be successful, students also need to feel they had some role in having developed those skills. Motivated students believe that they have the skills to do well in school and also recognize their own role in developing these skills (Siegle, 2012). Students who believe that their abilities are not innate but have been developed are more likely to attempt challenging tasks. Therefore, the strategies I will discuss in this chapter are designed to help students recognize that they are capable of doing well and achievement is under their control.

Sources of Efficacy

Past Performance

Self-efficacy beliefs generally are influenced by four sources of information: (a) one's own past performances, (b) the vicarious experience of observing models, (c) verbal persuasion, and (d) physiological clues (Bandura, 1986). The strongest of these is past experiences. Students who have been successful at a task in the past tend to believe they will be successful at similar tasks in the future. The opposite is also true. Students who have experienced a string of poor grades in a subject have probably convinced themselves that they are not good at that subject and do not expect to do well at it in the future. In fact, if given a choice, they avoid the subject at all cost. Because these past experiences have such a strong impact on how students view current and future tasks, educators and parents must help students recognize and appreciate their successes, however small they may be. Unfortunately, many underachievers focus on their poor performances, but fail to appreciate some of the small, positive steps they are making.

As an elementary student, I dreaded Wednesdays and Fridays. The weekly spelling pretest and final test were on Wednesday and Friday respectively. Each Monday, we received a list of 25 spelling words, and each Wednesday and Friday I traditionally misspelled 5 to 7 of them. I convinced myself that I was not good at spelling and did not put any effort into learning my weekly spelling words. It never occurred to me that the poor grades I was earning in spelling each week were caused by my lack of effort, rather than not having a natural ability. In some ways, low self-efficacy provides a student with an excuse for not doing well. This belief that I was not good at spelling was reinforced each week and became a self-fulfilling prophecy. The longer this pattern continues, the harder it is to break. Simply drawing the issue to the student's attention is ineffective.

Poor self-efficacy in one subject and the subsequent lack of effort and poor performance associated with it can carry over to other areas, and the student may begin to dread or dislike school in general. Interestingly, my academic performance in general dramatically improved in eighth grade, where spelling was not part of the curriculum. I no longer had a reason to dread school, and I began to embrace it.

Alternatively, success at a new task can sometimes blossom into strong self-efficacy and achievement. As a Ph.D. student, I enrolled in an advanced statistics course. One of the prerequisites for the course was a one-credit technology class on using the campus mainframe computer. (For those of you with an interest in technology, I have now revealed my age.) A friend suggested the class was not necessary, and I meekly enrolled without the required prerequisite. The first assignment required analyzing data with the campus mainframe. The instructor had prepared detailed instruction on how to do so and accompanied a group of us who were not familiar with the mainframe to the library to run our data. I successfully completed the task on the first attempt. The following week, I repeated my flawless performance. By the third week, I had become known as the statistics expert. Eventually I encountered a problem, and my code failed to run. I worked early into the morning hours problem solving and adjusting the programming code until the statistic ran correctly. I knew I could do it, and I believed if I stuck with it I would be successful. My self-efficacy at the task had been set, and a small setback did not detour my progress. Had that setback occurred during one of the first few weeks, I probably would have given up.

Vicarious Experiences

The second source of self-efficacy information is observing others similar to ourselves succeed or fail at a task. By observing others like themselves perform tasks, individuals make judgments about their own capabilities (Schunk, 1989b). If a student sees a friend publish a poem, he might believe he can also have one published. A third grader observing other third graders learning multiplication tables is likely to believe that she can also learn them. Unlike the self-efficacy beliefs derived from past experience, self-efficacy gained through observation is less stable. Once strong self-efficacy is developed from one's own personal successes, an occasional failure may not have negative effects; however, self-efficacy based on observing others succeed will diminish rapidly if the observers subsequently have unsuccessful experiences of their own.

Students who observe students similar to themselves succeed are likely to believe that they can perform as well as those students and thereby experience higher self-efficacy (Bandura, 1982). Models who are similar in competence provide the best opportunity for students to assess self-efficacy (Schunk, 1989a). When students observe peers succeed, particularly those they perceive as having lower skills than they do, they tend to believe they can be successful at similar tasks. However, if students observe peers fail, particularly those they perceive as being less talented than they, their confidence drops.

Although teachers are important models, other students can be at least as effective (Schunk & Hanson, 1985). For example, when elementary students are shown a video of peer models learning a skill, the observers gain more in self-efficacy and achievement than when they watch a video of a teacher. Predictably, both types of models are more effective than no model at all. The students relate to their peers' performance more, and the performance has an impact on them.

Hearing other students describe what they are doing while completing a task can positively affect the observer. When students observe their peers verbalize strategic steps, these students have higher self-efficacy and show stronger performance gains than students who do not have others verbalize their steps (Schunk & Rice, 1984). Verbalization prior to performing a task also has the same positive impact. The verbalizing draws attention to progress the student model is making, allowing other students to monitor progress and recognize their own achievement. Verbalization prior to a task functions as a vicarious experience in which the student experiences success before ever attempting the task.

An interesting line of research that maximizes perceived similarity to a model is *self-modeling*. In self-modeling, a video is made of a learner doing a task, focusing on positive behavior with negative or unsuccessful episodes edited out. For example, when elementary children view videos of their own mathematics work, they show better achievement than those who are recorded but do not see their videos, or those who are not recorded at all (Schunk & Hanson, 1989).

Viewing videos of peer models is not as useful as viewing oneself, but it results in greater skill acquisition than viewing no models at all. Video feedback showing one's own skillful performance conveys to students that they have made progress, and it increases their self-efficacy for that skill. In other words, it helps them recognize their successes.

Verbal Persuasion

A third source of information is verbal persuasion. If teachers tell students, "You can do this," it can also increase their confidence to do a task. Research about self-efficacy indicates that although verbal persuasion such as this can be important, it does not contribute as much as an individual's own experiences or vicarious experiences (Bandura, 1986). The short-term effects of persuasion need to be coupled with actual successes. The persuader's credibility is also an important factor with verbal persuasion (Schunk, 1989a). Students experience higher self-efficacy when someone they believe is trustworthy tells them they are capable. Students will also tend to discredit a teacher if they believe the teacher does not fully understand the demands of the task being faced. Despite verbal persuasion's limited effectiveness, teachers show a preference for it over using student models or accentuating students' past performances (Gorrell & Trentham, 1992). Parents and teachers can increase their students' confidence more if they help their students recognize past successes.

Interestingly, although positive verbal comments are not extremely effective, negative ones are deadly. One negative comment about a student's ability or performance can eclipse dozens of positive comments and even some past successes. Educators and parents must carefully monitor their comments to students.

Although there are many possible explanations for why one could fail, effort and ability are the most likely causes that students report (Good & Brophy, 1994). Students bring a wide variety of past experiences with them when they enter school. Some experiences have been positive; others have not. How students interpret their past successes and failures can have a dramatic impact on their self-efficacy, and the comments parents and educators make to students influence these perceptions.

With certain types of verbal feedback, teacher talk can have a significant effect on students' perceptions of their own effort and ability

(Schunk, 1984). Effort and ability are both internally perceived causes, according to attribution theory (Weiner, 1986), and the teacher's role can be to help students understand the relationship between effort and ability (Good & Brophy, 1994). This was discussed in Chapter 4.

Feedback, of course, is essential for learning and performance. Researchers increasingly find that feedback has many boundary conditions (Dweck, 1975; Schunk, 1989a). Feedback is not as simple as either "you receive it" or "you don't receive it"; rather, the style and content of feedback are also important. For example, Dweck (1975) found that, following failure, many students profited when teachers commented that the students didn't seem to be trying hard enough. Those students who anguished over their failure improved even more after they practiced the same explanation for failure: "I didn't put out enough effort." Dweck (1975) hypothesized that effort explanations are readily changeable because decisions about how much effort to expend are under personal control. By comparison, explanations that rely on more stable reasons, such as "I'm not good at this," are beyond personal control. If students blame failure on lack of ability, then they believe there is little that can be done to change the situation. Unfortunately, attributions for failure, practiced again and again, become self-fulfilling prophecies.

Physiological Clues

The final source of self-efficacy beliefs are physiological clues. Sweaty hands or a dry mouth are often interpreted as signs of nervousness (Bandura, 1986). Individuals may feel that such signs indicate they are not capable of succeeding at a particular task. Conversely, they may be aware of feeling relaxed before confronting a new situation and develop a higher sense of efficacy toward the task they face. Deep breathing exercises and relaxation techniques can possibly reduce tension prior to performing unfamiliar or difficult tasks and may help students maintain their confidence to perform them.

Making a Difference With Student Confidence: Motivation Tips to Recognize Growth

Our goal is to help students recognize that they have the ability to be successful. As stated in Chapter 4, students must also understand their abilities are malleable—they can improve with practice. Therefore, all efforts to help students recognize the skills they have developed should be coupled with language that also attributes their progress to effort on their part. Students' beliefs about how well they can perform are first and foremost influenced by how well they have performed in the past. Success breeds success. Significant adults in children's lives can increase students' confidence by helping them recognize past accomplishments. Helping students acknowledge past growth is an important contributor toward their future growth. Because past performance has the strongest influence on self-efficacy, parents and educators should create conditions where students have an opportunity to recognize their current and previous successes.

Videotape Students

Parents and educators can video record students as they are engaged in various activities. By periodically reviewing the recordings, students recognize how much they have improved. A young person who has been taking piano lessons for several years may not feel he has made any progress. Parents can videotape their child practicing and show it to him 6 months or one year later. The child will be amazed at how much better he plays. Without viewing the video, the child might not feel he had made any progress during that time period. This technique can be used with any activity where visible, but incremental, progress can be documented.

Maintain Student Portfolios

Educators and parents should keep samples of previous academic work and periodically review students' earlier work with them to show growth and improvement. Students are amazed at how easy their earlier work now appears and how much better they are now able to perform it. Student portfolios promote this type of self-reflection. Students can help select work to include in their portfolios for future review. Although it may seem strange, many students assume that school should become easier with each year. After all, they are learning the material, so classes should become easier. They fail to understand that an appropriate curriculum is one that will continually challenge them as they master it. Unfortunately, many young gifted students do not initially find school challenging. These students are particularly at risk of not expecting to be challenged in school and not believing that their efforts in school result in increased learning. By revisiting previous work, students can also develop an appreciation for the advances they are making.

Chart Progress

Teachers and parents can encourage students to compete with themselves by charting their progress. As previously noted, parents often reserve a special spot in their home to mark their children's height each year. Children love to observe how much they have grown. Just as parents chart height, educators and parents can also help children recognize other forms of growth and development. Teachers can record a running list of mastered spelling words or multiplication facts. Earlier in this chapter, I discussed my poor spelling performance. Each week I focused on the 5–7 words I had misspelled. I failed to recognize the 18–20 words I was spelling correctly each week. An effective strategy for turning my negative attitude about my spelling ability around might have been to chart the number of words I spelled correctly each week. Over the course of a grading period, I would have correctly spelled hundreds of words. Seeing a list of all the words I had correctly spelled would have helped me recognize I was making progress and learning to spell new words.

Discuss the Importance of Effort

As I noted in Chapter 4, Dweck (1999) demonstrated that students who believe abilities can be developed and are not fixed are more likely to attempt challenging tasks and persevere through difficulties than students who believe abilities are innate. Students who have a performance orientation approach new situations as opportunities to show what they know. These students tend to believe that abilities are fixed. Therefore, they view any mistakes as evidence that they lack ability. In contrast, students who have a mastery/learning orientation view new situations as opportunities to acquire new skills or improve their existing skills. Students with a mastery/learning orientation tend to believe that abilities are malleable, and they are more likely to tackle difficult tasks. Although Dweck (1999) found that students already gravitate toward one or the other of these orientations in elementary school, she also found that these orientations are amenable to change.

Gifted students are at risk of developing a performance orientation, which may limit their willingness to take academic risks. Gifted students often perceive giftedness as innate, and they may believe they had very little to do with their giftedness. Although it is true that gifted students often acquire skills more quickly and easily than their peers, they still gain such skills through learning. It is important for gifted students to recognize that the talents they possess are acquired, and they are capable of further developing these talents.

Gifted students also need to understand that just because they find something difficult does not mean they are not smart. For some students, not trying preserves an image. They do not perceive "not trying" as poor performance. They can always say, "It wasn't important" or "I just rushed through it and didn't do my best." Young people often believe that if they need to work hard at school, then they are not smart. Their peers hold a similar view of themselves and others.

Give Specific, Developmental Compliments

Attributing success to ability or effort is a fine line to walk. The key is to acknowledge ability while recognizing that effort went into its development. Educators and parents can help students recognize the important role both ability and effort play in talent development. One way to achieve this is through the comments made to children. As discussed in Chapter 4, the way we compliment students has an impact on how successful students perceive themselves to be. Everyone agrees that students should be encouraged to work hard, as effort plays a significant role in achievement. However, students also need to believe they have the skills to succeed. The key in complimenting students is to help them recognize that skills are developed, and they have acquired the skills necessary to succeed. The feedback must contain (a) recognition of the talent and (b) attribution of its development to the student.

Parents and educators should compliment students on the specific skills they have developed by drawing attention to the skill and to its development. This acknowledges the effort without drawing undue attention to it. These comments should be specific rather than general compliments. A general compliment such as, "Good work" doesn't carry the weight of something more specific such as, "You have really developed the ability to provide supporting sentences for the topic sentence in your paragraphs." Specific feedback allows students to better appraise their progress by letting them know two things: what specific skill they possess and how they developed it. Both components are necessary. Students will reflect on the comment and think, "Yes, I have learned to write a well-organized paragraph."

Avoid est

As I discussed in Chapter 6, Sylvia Rimm has cautioned educators and parents to avoid *est* words such as *best, greatest, finest, prettiest, fastest, strongest*, and so forth. Learning and growing are lifelong activities. Productive individuals realize they always have room to improve and there are always opportunities to learn new things. Students who hear they are the best, greatest, or finest may be less likely to adopt a mastery learning mindset and may begin to believe there are ceilings to achievement.

Introduce Performance Models

Educators and parents can arrange for models who can successfully perform skills to be learned. At first, this will likely be the teacher, parent, or another adult, but soon other students and peers who catch on quickly may be used as models. Tasks can be broken into smaller sections so peer models can be used as early as possible in a lesson.

Teachers and parents should consider a variety of ways to use models. Video recording is easy and effective, although editing video for self-modeling can be time consuming. Self-modeling can also occur through visualization. Before beginning a new task, educators and parents can mentally walk a student through the task. By talking the student or a class through the task first, students develop a sense of success before they even encounter the task. This strategy has been used successfully with students who are afraid of change. Before adults ask students they are working with to begin longer term projects, they should take a few minutes to review the project with the students. They can ask the students to share what steps they may take and how they see the final project. Peer tutoring, work groups, and class demonstrations can also help to exploit the power of models. As previously stated, students must perceive some similarity between themselves and the model. Therefore, the skill difference between peer models and themselves cannot be too large.

Camouflage Unsolicited Help

When teachers offer unsolicited advice or help to students, the students may believe the advice or help signals low ability on their part (Zimmerman & Martinez-Pons, 1990). Not only do the students being helped think of themselves as less capable, but other students watching the interaction come to the same conclusion. Expressing sympathy following a poor performance or praise after an easy task has the same effect and sends a low-ability cue (Graham & Barker, 1990). Even first graders attach importance to teacher feedback styles. They believe, for example, that teachers watch low achievers more and scold those they think could do better. Therefore, teachers should avoid asking a student if she is having trouble. Instead, the teacher can begin by saying, "I like your opening topic sentence. What kinds of examples will you give in the rest of the paragraph to support your position?" or "Yes, you see clearly the first step in this two-step math problem. How will you proceed to the second step?" In both of these examples, a common thread exists. First, the teacher begins with a positive comment on a real strength in the student's work. Second, without focusing on the student's ability, a question provides information about what additional avenues the student may want to explore. Third, the statements place responsibility for learning onto the student. The adult might also try a neutral invitation for help, "How are you doing?"

In a similar vein, some teachers do tend to focus on inappropriate behavior more than appropriate behavior so that students rightly believe that if a teacher approaches them, it is for something they did incorrectly rather than correctly. A 4:1 rule of more positive descriptive comments over negative ones has been suggested (Alberta Education, 2006).

Share Goals

A tried and true teaching practice is to tell students what they will be learning, teach them the material, and then tell them what they have learned. This strategy can be effectively implemented in a classroom to help all students recognize the progress the class is making. As a university professor, I teach a graduate course in educational research. The course includes an introduction to basic statistical concepts. The class usually intimidates beginning graduate students. Many of them are anxious about any topic associated with mathematics. Therefore, my first task is to build their self-efficacy about the course content. I begin each lesson by providing a list of topics that we will be covering during that class period. Although the list provides an excellent advanced organizer and helps keep me on track, its intended function is to draw students' attention to the content they are learning.

I project the list on the board, and as I finish each topic, draw attention to the topic on the list that has just been covered by placing a check next to it. At the end of class, we review each term on the list and discuss what we have learned. I usually begin the class by quickly reviewing the previous class list and presenting a new list. Throughout the semester, we refer back to these lists, and the students comment on how much they have learned.

None of these performance strategies works perfectly. However, a combination of them can begin to help students recognize the skills they have and the important role they play in developing these skills. Although this chapter provided some strategies for improving students' confidence in their ability to perform tasks, being confident about one's abilities is not sufficient. Students must also believe the task is important enough to put forth effort, and they must believe that others will support their efforts and will believe they can be successful. These issues are discussed in the next two chapters.

chapter 9

Goal Valuation

Making Learning More Meaningful

> *Goals are the fuel in the furnace of achievement.*
>
> —Brian Tracy

Students find their school tasks meaningful for a variety of reasons. These reasons will vary from one student to another, but they generally fall into four categories (Eccles & Wigfield, 1995). Some students see themselves as good students. They identify themselves as someone who does well in school, and this identity motivates them to work hard on whatever school-related tasks they encounter. Other students have a clear vision of their future and see the important role education plays in achieving their future aspirations. These students see school as a vehicle to future success. Another group of students does well in school when the topic interests them; student interest can be a powerful motivator for academic achievement (Siegle, Rubenstein, Pollard, et al., 2010). Finally, students do well when they see the immediate usefulness of the material they are learning. Perhaps they can apply the material directly to their lives, or perhaps they are simply being rewarded for doing well. Each of these examples represents a different reason why students would perceive their learning experiences as meaningful. For example, one student in a language arts class may work for top grades because she wants to attend a prestigious college or earn an important college scholarship. A second student may be hoping to become a writer and wants to sharpen his writing skills. A third student may simply enjoy writing. A fourth may be writing a blog and is applying what she is learning in language arts directly to her writing. Although each of these students is motivated to achieve in language arts, each is motivated to do well for a different reason.

When we (McCoach & Siegle, 2003a) compared the attitudes of gifted achievers and nonachievers, several interesting findings emerged. One of the more pertinent findings was the important role that valuing academic goals played in student motivation and achievement. Valuing the goals of school was more highly related to motivation than were students' attitudes toward school, attitudes toward teachers, or their academic self-perceptions. Unfortunately, many students do not see the importance of the material they are learning and do not find school meaningful. This can lead to academic underachievement. Our work with gifted underachievers (Rubenstein, Siegle, Reis, McCoach, & Burton, 2012; Siegle, 2012; Siegle et al., 2006) indicated that making school more meaningful for students who do not find it meaningful is among the most promising strategies for reversing academic underachievement. This chapter will feature a variety of strategies that have effectively helped make school meaningful for students. None of the strategies work perfectly with every student, but combinations of these strategies can help students see that the work they are doing is meaningful.

Curriculum Compacting

Unfortunately, the material many gifted students encounter in their classrooms is not meaningful because they have already mastered it. Sally Reis and her colleagues (1993) discovered that many gifted elementary students already know up to half of the material that they are encountering in their regular classrooms. Repetition of mastered content certainly is not meaningful, and unfortunately, the reward for many students who master coursework quickly is more of the same. It is little wonder that academically advanced students often report feeling bored and unchallenged (Plucker & McIntire, 1996). Instead of quickly completing the work they know they have already mastered, these advanced students sometimes become disenchanted; they mentally drop out, and fail to finish even the simplest of assignments.

Curriculum compacting is one of the most common forms of curriculum modification for academically advanced students. It is also the basic procedure upon which many other types of modification are founded. Compacting is based on the premise that those students who either demonstrate mastery of course content or have the potential to master course content more quickly can buy time to study material that they find more challenging and interesting (Renzulli & Reis, 1997).

Both basic skills, such as multiplication facts, and course content, such as how a bill becomes law, can be compacted. Although basic skills compacting is easier for teachers new to the process, the latter is probably more common in secondary schools. Basic skills compacting involves determining what basic skills students have mastered and eliminating the practice or repetition of those skills. For example, beginning chemistry students who have demonstrated mastery of the periodic table would have little need for further drill and practice in its use and would be better served by advancing to more complex course content.

Sometimes, academically advanced students may not have mastered course content, but they are capable of doing so at an accelerated pace. They may have some understanding of the content already and will require minimal time or instruction for mastery. In these cases, content compacting is useful. Perhaps a sophomore class is reading *To Kill a Mockingbird* and reflecting on the societal ramifications of racial prejudice. Some students read at a much faster rate and are able to cover the novel more quickly than others or are able to demonstrate mastery of the objectives associated with the novel. An incident with a former student of mine over his experience with the novel illustrates the importance of compacting.

Dean loved to read and was excited when his sophomore teacher distributed *To Kill a Mockingbird* on Friday afternoon. She assigned the first few chapters for weekend reading. Dean was scheduled to play an out-of-town basketball game that evening and decided to start reading the book on the bus trip to the game. He became engrossed in the story and finished reading the novel that evening after returning from the trip. Monday morning he reported to his literature teacher that it was a great book.

"You didn't finish it already," she commented, but after a short conversation, she was convinced he had.

"What are we reading next?" he asked. She gave him the next novel, and he finished it in a couple of days and asked for the next one.

She hesitated, "I don't want you mixing up the stories when we discuss them in class, so I'm not going to give you the next one."

He relayed the incident to me. "Mr. Siegle, I'm not going to mix up *To Kill a Mockingbird* with—," he said. He enjoyed the class discussion and didn't want to miss it; he simply wanted to continue reading interesting literature. This young man would have been a good candidate for content compacting.

I once explained compacting to a group of sixth-grade students who were part of a study being conducted by The National Research Center on the Gifted and Talented. One asked, "What is it again?" I explained that their teacher was planning to test them on their school material, and they would not be required to do worksheets or workbook pages for the material they already knew. One young girl looked at me rather puzzled and said, "Well, that just makes sense." Curriculum compacting does "just make sense." Each year thousands of students coast academically as they repeat material that they already have mastered or which they could easily master in a fraction of the time.

Imagine that you've just finished vacuuming your home, and your partner arrives. After complimenting you on how nice the house looks, your partner suggests that you vacuum it again. When you question your partner, he or she responds that you might forget how to vacuum and you ought to practice. After you refuse, your partner tells a friend that he or she can't understand why you didn't want to vacuum the house again. Your partner notes that he or she knows that you know how to vacuum but can't understand why you "just won't do it." Although this story may seem absurd, many educators have heard teaching colleagues complain about a student who knows how do a particular worksheet or homework assignment, but "just won't do it." Perhaps, like the vacuuming incident, if the student has demonstrated that he or she knows the material, it doesn't need to be repeated again.

The compacting procedure is simple: Determine what the students already know and what they still need to learn, then replace what they know with more challenging material that they would like to learn (Starko, 1986). Generally, two basic principles are recommended when compacting. First, grades should be based on the material compacted (what the student has mastered) rather than the replacement material. Students may be reluctant to tackle more challenging material if they risk receiving lower grades that may reduce their chances for academic scholarships. This is not to say that replacement activities should not be evaluated. Second, replacement material should be based on student interests. Because replacement material will require greater student effort, the task commitment and responsibility necessary to work independently (which is often, but not always, the learning situation) mandate that the student has a vested interest in the content. There are eight basic steps to curriculum compacting:

1. Determine the learning objectives for the material.
2. Find an appropriate way to assess those objectives.
3. Identify students who may have already mastered the objectives (or could master them more quickly).
4. Assess those students to determine their mastery level.
5. Streamline practice or instruction for students who demonstrate mastery of the objectives.
6. Provide small-group or individual instruction for students who have not yet mastered all of the objectives, but are capable of doing so more quickly than their classmates.
7. Offer more challenging academic alternatives based on student interest.
8. Maintain a record of the compacting process and instructional options provided (Reis, Burns, & Renzulli, 1992).

Educators new to the process should consider the following recommendations:

- ❧ Start with one or two responsible students.
- ❧ Select content with which they feel comfortable.
- ❧ Try a variety of methods to determine student mastery of the material (a brief conversation with a student may be just as effective as a written pretest).
- ❧ Compact by topic rather than time.
- ❧ Define proficiency based on a consensus with administrators and parents.
- ❧ Don't be afraid to request help from available sources such as community volunteers (Reis et al., 1992).

Curriculum compacting works best when adopted by a school district as a regular part of good teaching practices. When superintendents, principals, and other administrators support and encourage the process, it is certainly much easier.

Teaching Appreciation of Learning

Curriculum specialist Sandra Kaplan (2006) has suggested that educators and parents can make learning more meaningful by teaching an appreciation of learning. Appreciation is achieved by teaching students (a) what came before, (b) what was happening at the same time, and (c) what were the effects of whatever is being learned. As a former professional photographer, I sit in awe of the progress that has been made with digital photography. Each fall I teach a university freshman honors seminar on increasing personal creativity through digital photography. Most of the university students in my class have never known a time without digital cameras; the idea of film and darkrooms is completely foreign to them. There is little wonder they do not share my passion and appreciation for the digital process.

The students begin to appreciate the digital process once they understand the lengthy and technical process necessary to produce photographs with film and chemicals. Their appreciation grows as they learn about the 50-year search to find a replacement for the precious metal, silver, used in the photographic process. Finally, once the students are exposed to the digital enhancement techniques made available by the new imaging medium, they begin to truly appreciate something they had taken for granted. Kaplan's (2006) steps for teaching appreciation for learning work well; however, they do require educators to have a firm understanding of the content they are teaching and the historical context in which it lies.

Nearly every educator has heard a young person ask, "Why do we have to learn this stuff?" Kaplan (2006) has suggested adults can discuss the importance of learning material with two simple questions. The first question is, "How will your life be different if you don't learn it?" Students who do not value something probably cannot envision their lives being any different without the knowledge being discussed. However, with a little conversation, some useful reasons may surface. Kaplan's second question is even more powerful. "How might your life be different if you do learn it?" Knowledge is a powerful tool that creates opportunities. Many young people fail to see future possibilities due to their limited experiences. Taking the time to hold a thoughtful discussion with young people about the advantages and disadvantages of having mastered certain material can teach them an appreciation of learning that makes school content more meaningful. Additionally, when introducing a complex topic, teachers can refer to it as "interesting" and "intriguing" rather than as "difficult."

Five Cs That Encourage Learning

Kanevsky and Keighley (2003) interviewed gifted students who were bored and disengaged in high school. What they learned from their research is useful for making school more meaningful. First, they discovered that learning is the opposite of and the antidote to boredom. James Gallagher and his colleagues (1997) have noted that gifted students generally enjoy learning and do not want to be bored in school. They often equate lack of challenge with boredom (Gallagher et al., 1997). Kanevsky and Keighley proposed five Cs that encourage learning.

Kanevsky and Keighley (2003) found that gifted high school students sought some *control* or self-determination, which enabled them to have *choices*. These choices involved enhancing the "relevance of the content and connections between the curriculum, their interests, and real world experiences" (Kanevsky & Keighley, 2003, p. 23). It also involved creating more *challenge* with higher level thinking, a quicker pace, and experience with authentic material. These combined for a *complexity* that included "rich, messy content, processes that involved high level thinking and questioning, their emotions and interests, opportunities to develop sophisticated products using the resources of a professional and opportunities to work in professional contexts" (Kanevsky & Keighley, 2003, p. 24). Finally, the students sought *caring* teachers. The researchers noted that a caring teacher could compensate for the first four Cs. In the next section, I will discuss how these factors create intellectually stimulating learning experiences.

Promote Intellectual Stimulation

Beginning with my first training on working with gifted students, I was taught the importance of providing gifted students with academic challenge. I was told that gifted students were often bored in class because they already knew much of the material, and I needed to create academically challenging tasks. As I worked with students, I soon discovered they did not always embrace the academically challenging tasks I created. One day, while I was talking with my future wife on the phone, a revelation occurred that has changed my approach to teaching and learning. She was exploring potential doctoral programs, and I suggested that she consider the program where I received my degree. Upon further reflection, I had second thoughts about my suggestion. She had already read most of the available literature on gifted students. Just for fun, she had also completed several semesters of advanced statistics. I became concerned that she was entering the doctoral program with as much knowledge as I had gained when I left the program. I told her that I was concerned that she might not find the program academically challenging because of her previous experiences. She replied, "I don't want to be academically challenged." I was surprised and disappointed in her statement, but her next response restored my faith in her passion for learning. She continued, "I want to be intellectually stimulated." That phrase still plays in my mind years later and has changed my understanding of learning needs.

Like my wife, all of us desire intellectual stimulation. Providing gifted students with academic challenge is not sufficient—what they seek is intellectual stimulation. Academic challenge is a part of intellectual stimulation, but intellectual stimulation involves more. Although academic challenge may be a quest for mastery, intellectual stimulation is a search for meaning. The relationship between academic challenge and intellectual stimulation is interesting. Too little academic challenge and too little intellectual stimulation produce bored students. Too much academic challenge and too little intellectual stimulation produce "turned off" students. Too much academic challenge with adequate intellectual stimulation produces frustrated students. Optimal challenge combined with intellectual stimulation produces students who are motivated and learning. Deci and Ryan (1985) found that students are intrinsically motivated to pursue activities that are moderately novel, interesting, enjoyable, exciting, and optimally challenging. Material that is either too hard or too easy is anti-motivational. When schoolwork is too easy, students become bored; when tasks are too difficult, students become frustrated and anxious.

So, how do we promote intellectual stimulation? Kanevsky and Keighley's (2003) Cs provide a clue as to the type of intellectual stimulation that bored students are seeking. As previously stated, challenge certainly is a factor, but that challenge needs to be relevant. It can be tied to students' interests, or it can also be tied to authentic learning and real-world experiences. Joseph Renzulli (1982) has long been a proponent of providing talented students with opportunities to create authentic products or services for authentic audiences. In his and Sally Reis's Schoolwide Enrichment Model (Renzulli & Reis, 1997), students are encouraged to implement the authentic methodologies of practicing professionals to create "real products" that bring change to "real audiences." When I asked students to write stories, the quality of their work varied. When the students learned their stories were to be bound in a book (*an authentic product*), they usually wanted to rework their stories and make them better. When the students learned the book would be catalogued into the school library for other students to check out and read (*an authentic audience*), they often elected to edit the work once again to improve the quality. Educators and parents should not underestimate the power of having students do authentic learning that culminates in authentic products or services for authentic audiences. This involves using resources and techniques similar to practicing professionals. The effort and care students put into their work are directly related to the exposure their work receives and the work's importance as perceived by the students and those around them.

Higher order thinking and questioning can also promote intellectual stimulation. Searching for questions to ask, as well as searching for the answers to those questions, inspires intellectual interest. Unanswered questions promote discussion, usually involve big ideas, often have no content ceiling, offer multiple perspectives, and encourage higher levels of cognition. Working on problems that have multiple answers and multiple paths to a single answer is usually more interesting than applying a tried and true algorithm.

Recognize Student Interests

Intellectual stimulation also occurs when students are passionate about what they are learning. Students are passionate about topics that interest them. Educators and parents should never underestimate the role interest plays in achievement; interest is one of the strongest self-reported predictors of achievement across a wide variety of domains (Siegle, Rubenstein, Pollard, et al., 2010). Students should be given opportunities to explore their interests in and out of school. Parents can help students apply students' interests to school projects, and teachers can learn students' interests and incorporate them into the curriculum they are teaching and the instructional strategies they are using. Whenever possible, teachers should offer students authentic choices about the ways in which students can learn and show mastery of the material in the class. Teachers may want to ask students for ideas about alternative projects or products. The choices students make are often related to their interests.

Explain Why

The well-known educational psychologist Jere Brophy (2008) noted that:

> for much of what we teach in school, especially the more abstract content and higher order processes, the reasons for learning it are not obvious to students, and sometimes not even to teachers. This analysis highlights situations in which what is taught is worth learning, but students may not appreciate its value unless their learning is scaffolded in ways that help them to do so. (p. 134)

Therefore, an important step toward making school more meaningful for students is for educators to ask themselves, "Why am I teaching this, and how can I help my students see its importance?" Educators should explain the purpose for lessons and assignments. At the beginning of every unit, teachers can explain why mastering a set of skills or learning certain information is important to (a) help students meet their own current needs or wants, (b) provide students with social rewards or opportunities for social advancement, or (c) prepare students for occupational or other future successes (Brophy, 1998). Before every lesson, teachers can briefly state why students are learning about a given topic and explain how it is useful in one or two sentences.

Set Goals

More than a century ago, Friedrich Nietzsche noted, "the future influences the present just as much as the past." What students wish to achieve in the future certainly influences the effort they place on current tasks. Teachers can help students set short- and long-term academic goals. Short-term goals work better for younger students; however, regardless of the students' ages, it is essential that the goals are meaningful to the students themselves. Goals that adults value may have little meaning to children. Educators can encourage students to think seriously about how their performance in present classes can affect their future goals, as well as to articulate explicitly their reasons for choosing or failing to put forth effort in a class. Educators can help students see beyond the present activity to the long-term benefits it produces. A school assignment may seem unimportant, but acceptance into a prestigious university, a lucrative college scholarship, or a rewarding occupation may be outcomes that students value. Teachers can invite community members into the classroom, and such individuals can tie school curriculum to their career activities. Parents can also share how they use various skills they learned in school (Siegle & McCoach, 2005b).

Consider Rewards

Everyone seems to have an opinion on the benefits or evils of rewards, and research studies abound to support each view. Rewards are neither inherently good nor bad; their appropriateness and effectiveness depend on the situation. External rewards can produce negative consequences when used with students who are already intrinsically motivated to perform a task. If a student is motivated to do well, then introducing an external reward system can sometimes sidetrack that motivation. For example, Jon was a student who loved to read. He was a voracious reader and spent much of his spare time reading for pleasure. His school implemented a reading reward program to encourage students to read. Each book in the school library was assigned points that students could earn for reading it, and reading difficult books earned students more points. Students at the school received various prizes for collecting points. Jon soon learned that he could read several lower-point-value books in the time it took to read one challenging book, and the combination of the lower-point-value books exceeded the high score for reading one challenging book. Jon was intent on collecting the most points of anyone in his school, and he quickly went about reading scores of easy, lower-point-value books. The extrinsic rewards of the reading program actually decreased Jon's intrinsic motivation to read challenging and interesting books. Although the program had negative consequences for Jon, it also had positive consequences for some of the reluctant readers who discovered a joy in reading after becoming involved in the program.

External rewards can be useful for students who may not be intrinsically motivated to do well. When I was a gifted and talented coordinator, we identified Tari for our gifted program based on her test data. She had been receiving average grades, but the identification data indicated that she was a bright child who should be a top student. When we approached Tari's parents—one of whom was a teacher in our school system—about placing Tari in the program, they were reluctant. They felt their older child was far more gifted, and Tari had only average ability. We persuaded the parents to enroll Tari in the program for a trial period.

A Dairy Queen was located two blocks from our school. As a reward for doing well, I offered students who earned outstanding grades a trip to the Dairy Queen with a friend for Blizzard ice cream treats. The school principal had approved the idea, and students enjoyed bringing a friend along for their special rewards. At the end of the first marking period, Tari had earned all A's, and she, her friend, and I walked to the Dairy Queen and enjoyed Blizzard treats. Tari earned Blizzards for the four marking periods that year. She went on to become an outstanding student and graduated at the top of her class.

Several years later, Tari's father commented on how effective the enrichment program was in turning Tari's achievement around. I smiled and thanked him, but thought to myself, "Blizzards turned Tari's achievement around." The Blizzard reward motivated Tari to embrace learning. The success she experienced increased not only her confidence to do well in school, but her enjoyment of school. When the Blizzard rewards stopped, Tari continued to achieve.

My associates in the school psychology program often use a reward program called Mystery Motivators to challenge students. The program has two key features: (1) A jar is created with various simple rewards, and (2) the student provides input into what some of the rewards might be. For example, a student who was sent to the office several times a week wanted to go fishing at a stream near the school during lunchtime with the science teacher if he went a week without being sent to the office. The science teacher agreed, and a slip of paper with the fishing trip was put in the Mystery Motivator jar. Other rewards might include a free homework pass, a small treat, or free time. Students are neither fully aware of all of the rewards that are placed in the jar, nor do they know how many of each reward are available. The mystery factor is necessary to avoid having students only perform well when a desired reward is available. Thus, the reward is only revealed once students have reached the goal they set, and students hold out hope that their favorite reward will be drawn.

Naturally, the goal is to slowly wean students from external rewards as they develop achievement habits and become intrinsically motivated. A second jar can be used to regulate the frequency of the rewards. For example, a combination of red and green marbles could be placed in the jar. When goals are met, a marble is drawn to determine whether a reward will be given. Green marbles represent reward days and red marbles represent days without rewards. The ratio of green to red marbles can change as the program progresses. Initially, the jar contains more green marbles, but as students begin to internalize the positive actions, the need for rewards decreases, and the ratio favors red marbles. Some teachers do not share the color ratio and place the marbles in a wrapped jar.

As we have discovered in this chapter, students find school meaningful for a variety of reasons, and no single strategy is effective with all learners. Learning what motivates students, however, is the first step to modifying the curriculum and the learning environment for them. Educators and parents can use students' responses to the following statements to obtain a more complete picture of what factors students find meaningful:

1. When I try hard in this class, it's because _____

   _____.

2. I would spend more time on my schoolwork if _____

   _____.

3. If I do poorly in this class, then _____

   _____.

4. When I don't try hard in this class, it's because _____

   _____.

5. I would rather do _____

   than do my work for this class.

6. Doing well in this class will help me to _____

   _____.

7. Doing poorly in this class will keep me from _____

   _____.

8. This class is important because _____

   _____.

9. The thing that I am most interested in learning more about

   is _____.

10. The most interesting thing that I learned in this class is

    _____.

Based on the pattern of information learned from these responses, educators and parents can explore some of the strategies presented in this chapter to make school more meaningful for reluctant learners.

chapter 10

Environmental Perceptions

Building Trusting Relationships

Whatsoever the mind has ordained for itself, it has achieved.

—Seneca

Students' perceptions of their environment play an important role in their achievement motivation. Students must expect to succeed and should know that those around them will support their efforts. They must trust that their efforts will not be thwarted by external factors and believe that putting forth effort is not a waste of time and energy. Students who view their environment as friendly and reinforcing may be more likely to demonstrate motivated behavior. Phrases such as "My teacher does not like me" or "I cannot learn the way he teaches" may be signs that students do not view their environment as friendly or that they have developed a belief that their efforts do not affect outcomes (Rathvon, 1996).

Some environmental factors are within an individual's control whereas others are not. As noted earlier, Ogbu (1978) showed that people put their effort into areas where they believe they can be successful and in environments where they believe they are supported. Thus, perceptions of the environment factor significantly in achievement motivation. Believing one has the skills to do well and believing the task is important are necessary components for an achievement attitude, but they are not sufficient. Students must also believe their efforts are supported rather than stifled. As previously stated, engagement and performance are based on the interaction of self-efficacy, task meaningfulness, and environmental perceptions. In this chapter, I will discuss factors related to environmental perceptions: how students perceive the support they are or are not receiving.

Relationships With Teachers

Students overwhelmingly attribute their interest and motivation to their experiences with their teachers. Students' perceptions of school and their teachers have an impact on students' academic attitudes and behaviors. It is important to emphasize the perception component of this concept; the environmental factor does not have to be true for the students to believe it is true and, therefore, for it to affect their motivation and behaviors. This is a particularly important concept of which teachers should be aware; even if teachers believe they are supporting students, if the students perceive otherwise, students will be less likely to try. Gifted students perceive a supportive environment when they build positive relationships with their teachers and when they feel their teachers are knowledgeable enough to teach them (Siegle, Rubenstein, & Mitchell, 2010).

Meaningful Relationships

Gifted achievers find teachers to be inspiring when they foster meaningful relationships with their students. This includes when teachers demonstrate that they care about their students, know them personally, and are interested in helping them succeed. One way teachers can connect with their students is through humor. For example, humor in lecture can help students pay attention. Students appreciated when their teachers "joked around with them" (Siegle, Rubenstein, & Mitchell, 2010). Humor seems to help students stay motivated and interested in the course and solidifies a connection between students and the teacher. Not everyone does humor well. It comes naturally for some of us and not so naturally for others, so educators should proceed with caution when attempting humor.

Educators can further demonstrate that they care in a variety of ways, including attending student activities, learning students' outside interests, and putting students' names in the problem sets on tests. My seventh-grade students loved seeing their names in the test questions. As a twist, I exchanged the first letters of their first and last name. For example, my name would be Sel Diegle. Although it took minimal effort, they looked forward to seeing how I might manipulate their names or use them on the next test. However, relationship building is challenging because it falls along a continuum. If a teacher is too distant, it has negative consequences on students' desire to engage with the class, but the other end of the continuum can be just as dangerous. Teachers can cross a fine line by trying to be too friendly. Our research (Siegle, Rubenstein, & Mitchell, 2010) found that students want caring teachers, but not teachers who are "too buddy buddy."

Knowledgeable Teachers

In addition to forming positive social relationships, gifted students also want to be assured that their teacher is knowledgeable. If they do not believe the teacher knows more than they, it has a detrimental effect on their desire to do well in a class. Poor content knowledge limits the number of instructional strategies that are available to teachers; such teachers do not stray from the textbook or venture into discussions with their students because doing so might lead them into unfamiliar territory. These teachers tend to stick with prepared lectures that feature little variety.

Students also appreciate teachers who can show how the information they are teaching connects with other disciplines. These cross-disciplinary connections make for interesting learning. Therefore, it is not only important for teachers to have expertise in the subject area they are teaching, but it is also important for them to have a strong foundation of knowledge across disciplines.

Bias-Free Teachers

Students must believe their teachers have the knowledge and skills to teach them. They need to perceive that their teachers are capable of teaching them something new and interesting. It goes without saying that students must also believe their teachers are treating them fairly. Some teachers do not appreciate gifted and talented students because they may see them as threatening or privileged. Students sense these not-so-hidden resentments and sometimes "write off" these teachers. This disengagement can lead to underachievement.

Historically, Americans have held ambivalent attitudes toward gifted students and gifted education (Begin & Gagné, 1994a). The tension between excellence and equity has a long history in the American educational system (Gallagher, 1994). Although people prize achievement and creative productivity, they despise making distinctions between superiority and inferiority in academic, political, or social domains. In their reworking of Tannenbaum's (1962) classic study of students' attitudes toward the gifted, Cramond and Martin (1987) asked preservice and in-service teachers to complete an attitude questionnaire that assessed participants' attitudes toward students who were athletic/non-athletic, brilliant/non-brilliant, and studious/non-studious. Both preservice and in-service teachers gave the highest ratings to average-non-studious-athletic students and gave the lowest ratings to brilliant-studious-non-athletic students.

Michener (1980) found that those who perceive themselves as academically gifted or who have gifted friends and family tend to harbor more positive attitudes toward the gifted. In addition, contact with gifted children, past participation in a gifted program, the presence of a gifted program in the participant's school, and perceived knowledge of giftedness have been significant predictors of attitudes toward the gifted in the majority of studies that included these variables (Begin & Gagné, 1994a, 1994b). Attitudes toward the gifted can also be influenced by the availability of and competition for resources. For example, McCoach and Siegle (2007) found that special education teachers showed poorer attitudes toward gifted students than other groups. They hypothesized the reason might be competition for school resources.

Active Listening

Understanding a student's perspective is a key component in addressing environmental perception issues. Active listening is a simple strategy that parents and educators can use to communicate with students. Active listening is a technique where the listener paraphrases back to the speaker what he or she believes the speaker has said. This assures that both the listener and the speaker understand one another. It allows the listener to clarify what is being said, and it allows the speaker an opportunity to work through an issue.

The steps of active listening are:

- providing verbal or nonverbal awareness of the other person (e.g., eye contact);
- responding to a person's basic verbal message;
- reflecting feelings, experiences, or content that has been heard or perceived through cues;
- offering a tentative interpretation about the other person's feelings, desires, or meanings;
- bringing together feelings and experiences in some way, providing a focus;
- questioning in a supportive way that requests more information or that attempts to clear up confusions;
- sharing perceptions of the other person's ideas or feelings, disclosing relevant personal information;
- showing warmth and caring in one's own individual way;
- discovering whether interpretations and perceptions are valid and accurate; and
- giving the other person time to think as well as to talk (Pickering, 1986).

For example, a student might return from school, slam the door, and announce, "I hate school." This provides a great opportunity to actively listen. The parent might respond, "So you don't like school?"

Student: "My teacher doesn't like me."

Parent: "You think your teacher does not like you?"

Student: "She kept me in during recess."

Parent: "You weren't allowed to go outside for recess today?"

Student: "I didn't do my homework last night, and she made me stay in for recess to finish it."

This short dialogue illustrates how active listening can be used to discover the core issue that may be bothering a student. Those who actively listen should be genuinely interested in learning what is bothering the student. The listener should also avoid being judgmental. The goal is to keep the lines of communication open to help the students work through the troubling issue and to understand what is troubling the student.

Stereotype Threat

Environmental perceptions go beyond the classroom. Cultural and economic factors may also be limiting student opportunities. Students' perceptions about the fairness of "the system" or of society in general impact their motivation. Steele (2000) reported that students may have difficulty trusting the environment; their achievement may be less influenced by their perceived abilities than by their perception of the fairness of the environment. Steele randomly assigned a group of students to one of two groups. He told one group that individuals with their characteristic did not do as well on a given task as individuals without this characteristic, but he said nothing to the other group that also possessed the characteristic. He asked both groups to perform a task. Those who were told that they possessed the referential characteristic performed much worse on the task than those for whom nothing was stated. Steele labeled the phenomenon *stereotype threat*.

"Stereotype threat" is the predicament students experience when evaluated in a situation where a negative cultural stereotype about their group's intellectual abilities is relevant. Because of the nature of stereotyping in this country, Black and Latino students face this predicament very often; girls and women face it in the traditionally male-dominated domains of math and physical sciences. . . . Over 200 published studies show that the experience of stereotype threat can undermine test performance, and over time, interfere with students' long-term academic performance and development. (Aronson & Juarez, 2012, p. 20)

Stereotype threat does not affect every member of a designated group. Individuals must internalize it, and their association with the stereotyped group must be manifest. For example, asking females to indicate their gender on a mathematics test can activate it. A group of Black students in a homogenous group may not suffer from it, but a few Black students in a group of White students might (Aronson & Juarez, 2012). However, stereotype threat is a very real factor in many students' lives. In addition to ethnic and cultural stereotypes, students who hear that they "grew up on the wrong side of the tracks" or have come from families where "nobody ever amounted to anything" certainly are at risk. There is some evidence that stereotype threat begins to more strongly exert an influence around grade 6. However, Aronson and Juarez (2012) cautioned that "behavior and emotions are most likely to be determined by current active mindsets—what a person believes at a given moment—rather than longstanding attitudes that are measured by questionnaires . . . remove[d] from the situation in question" (p. 31).

Stroessner, Good, and Webster (n.d.) offered some suggestions for limiting stereotype threat, which include:
- ❧ reframing the task,
- ❧ deemphasizing threatened social identities,
- ❧ encouraging self-affirmation,
- ❧ emphasizing high standards with assurances of capability,
- ❧ providing role models,

ℒ proving external attributions for difficulty, and

ℒ emphasizing an incremental view of ability.

Reframing the task involves reducing stereotype threat by using different language to describe the task. For example, assuring females that a mathematics test is gender fair can alleviate stereotype threat in a testing situation. Simply placing requests for demographic information at the end of a test can deemphasize threatened social identities. Each of us holds various identities, and helping students identify a nonthreatened social identity can also be effective. Students can affirm their self-worth by thinking of characteristics, skills, and values that are important to them. Cohen, Garcia, Apfel, and Master (2006) showed that students who self-affirmed their worth by writing a brief essay describing what values were important to them earned better grades than students who did not. Emphasizing the importance of high standards and assuring students they are capable removes the judgment factor that activates stereotype threat. Role models who demonstrate proficiency in a domain can reduce stereotype threat for others. Stereotype threat can also be reduced by providing students with external attributions. For example, explaining to students that the environment is noisy and that it might be hard to concentrate can disarm the stereotype threat. Finally, helping students understand the malleable nature of abilities, as discussed in Chapter 4, has also been shown to reduce stereotype threat. When educators frame activities as opportunities to learn rather than checks of ability, they can change a situation from being a potential threat into a possibly vitalizing challenge (Alter, Aronson, Darley, Rodriguez, & Ruble, 2010).

Teach Options for Success

Trusting the environment also includes knowing how to function within it. Successful individuals use three strategies when faced with a difficult situation. In some situations, they change the environment to fit their needs. In other situations, they adjust their behavior to be successful in the existing environment. Finally, they may realize that the situation is a lost cause, abandon it entirely, and start over (Sternberg, 2001). Successful individuals ascertain which option is most likely to help them reach their goal.

When students are not successful in an environment, they need to ask themselves, "Is there something I could be doing to be more successful here?" If the answer is "No," the next question is, "Is there some way I can have the situation changed so that it works for me?" This involves collaborating with others to make changes. If the answer is "No," the final question is, "Can I be more successful somewhere else?" As Sternberg (2001) has noted, wisdom is knowing which of these options leads to success. Of course, individuals must want to be successful for this strategy to work.

A student with whom I worked was accustomed to being given choices. From an early age, his parents had offered him choices. If he were told to complete the odd mathematics problems, he would reply that he wanted to do the even. I soon learned that he would tackle challenging work as long as he had choices. Therefore, I would give him two choices, both challenging, and he would be content to select one and tackle the work. Our relationship worked well, and he was productive. Unfortunately, his fourth-grade teacher insisted that he needed to learn that life did not always offer choices. He reacted to her stance by simply refusing to do work. The teacher contacted his parents, and they promised to monitor his homework, but he refused to submit it.

One week, the conflict rose to a climax when the teacher announced that the student would stay after school on Friday afternoon and complete any work he had not finished during the week. The teacher informed the parents about the requirement. The week progressed, and the student did not complete any of his homework. When he started to leave on Friday afternoon, his teacher told him he needed to stay and complete the work. He sat at his desk and stared at his teacher while she corrected papers and prepared for the next week's class. She soon wanted to leave for the weekend, but was stuck. A more experienced teacher might not have put herself in this situation, but she was in it. She said he could not leave until the work was completed, and he had not finished any of the work. Interestingly, the student resolved the crisis. After sitting for several hours, he reached into his book bag and produced all of the work for the week, which he had been secretly completing. He put it on her desk and asked her to correct it. He had purposefully been keeping her after school, and he believed he had won. Needless to say, she did not respond well. The stalemate continued for the entire year; the young man refused to change his behavior to be successful in the classroom, and the teacher refused to provide choices for the student to be successful. The wise decision might have been to move him to a different classroom, but we did not have that option at the time. Interestingly, the young man ultimately did learn to compromise, later attended a prestigious university, and is successful in life. Unfortunately, fourth grade was not a pleasant experience for him or his teachers.

Educators and parents can help students understand when it is important "to stand their ground," when compromise might better serve their interests, or when ignoring or changing the situation is the best course of action.

Role Models for Underserved Populations

Underserved populations are a group of students who are at more risk for underachievement. Economic pressure to support the family, a lack of a strong educational tradition, and negative stereotypes are often cited as reasons for underachievement and reduced commitment to education (White, Sanbonmatsu, Croyle, & Smittipatana, 2002). White et al. (2002) proposed that some underserved populations may limit their efforts to maintain the acceptance of their peers. They found that participants performed below their capability when in the presence of someone they valued and who had struggled with a similar task. For these students, underachievement is a strategy they use to fit into the environment. Programs that provide underserved students with opportunities to interact with achieving, motivated peers may diminish this behavior. Rimm (1995) has stressed the importance of role models in achievers' lives, and this is extremely important when working with gifted students from underserved populations. Students need to observe others like themselves working hard and being successful.

Identifying Distortions

Many adolescents hold negative and inaccurate automatic thoughts or distortions, which fall into five categories (Greene, 2001):

- perceptions about what events occur (e.g., "The teacher doesn't like me, so she asks me lots of questions in class to put me on the spot."),
- attributions about why events occur (e.g., "I'm not doing as well as I could because the teacher grades too hard.")
- expectancies or predictions of what will occur (e.g., "I'll never earn an A from her."),
- assumptions about the nature of the world and correlations among events (e.g., "Adults don't listen to kids."), and
- beliefs about what "should" be (e.g., "I ought to be allowed to drop math if I don't like it.").

Greene (2001) suggested that to determine whether or not a particular cognition is faulty, parents and teachers can ask two questions:

- *How valid is the perception?* For example, if students report that they are bored because the curriculum is unchallenging, and an investigation determines that the curriculum is, in fact, not suitable, then this is not a faulty perception even if it is a contributing factor to students' underachievement.
- *How reasonable is it as an explanation for events?* For example, if students report that nothing less than a perfect grade is acceptable, or that a teacher is "out to get them," one should question the reasonableness of the statement.

Parents and educators need to work with students to clarify the students' perceptions, address whether those perceptions are accurate or distorted, and then address the issue. If they are accurate, the question to address is, "What would it take for you to do well?" This may involve changing the curriculum, classroom environment, or interactions with the teacher. The options for success (Sternberg, 2001) that I discussed earlier can be applied.

If the perception is a distortion, then active listening may be useful to unearth the core issue. Additionally, Greene (2001) suggested the following questions be included as parents and educators work through the active listening:

- How is this a problem for you?
- How controllable is this?
- To what extent can you change this?
- What would you like to change?
- How can we help you make this change?

The focus should be on what is occurring in the present and on how to actively change it for the future. It can be useful to explore exceptions to the problem so as to encourage the student to keep doing what is already working. Parents and educators can ask the following questions to address possible solutions (Greene, 2001):

- What is working for you now? How could you do more of the same?
- What are you doing that keeps this problem going? What would you rather be doing instead of your problem?
- What would you like to try that is different from what you usually do?
- What kinds of problems have you previously solved? How?
- When you had a problem like this one before, what good solutions did you work out? If you have never had this type of problem before, have you ever helped someone else with this type of problem?
- What changes did you make that were better than those you are making now?

- ✋ What were the times when you expected to have this problem and you did not actually have it, or you dealt well with it?
- ✋ What solutions have worked well for you, and what ones have not?
- ✋ When you stopped feeling upset/angry/frustrated/incapable, what had you done to make yourself stop?
- ✋ What interrupted your problem and made it better or tolerable?

Students must believe that those around them value them and want to see them succeed. Their perceptions of their environment can either spur them to work hard or dishearten them. Not all students live in an academically supportive environment, and students need caring teachers and parents who believe they have the ability to do well. They need peers who support academic excellence. Students who are not encouraged to be successful or are not expected to be academic achievers are less motivated to achieve (Long-Mitchell, 2011). Students' attitudes toward school and achievement orientation influence their achievement behaviors and motivation (Ford, 1996). Their beliefs about the relationship between schooling and future success also influence academic performance (Sanders, 1998). Students' perceptions of school and home events; the nature of teachers' and parents' expectations and support; and the patterns of interaction between students, teachers, and parents have an impact on their academic attitudes and behaviors.

chapter 11

Developing Self-Regulation and Study Skills

The secret of all great undertakings is hard work and self-reliance.
—Gustavus F. Swift

When students have positive attitudes in the three areas of self-efficacy, task meaningfulness, and environmental perceptions, they set realistic goals and self-regulate to "get the job done." When any one of these three attitudes is low, students can fail to engage and achieve. Some (Ruban & Reis, 2006) have suggested that teaching gifted students study skills and self-regulation strategies promotes academic achievement. Although I acknowledge that these skills are important, my experience in working with gifted students has shown that making school more meaningful appears to be the most effective strategy to address student underachievement with gifted students. Many gifted students have the skills to be successful; they simply are not choosing to engage and apply those skills because they do not see the meaningfulness in the tasks they are being asked to do.

In recent research (Siegle, Rubenstein, & McCoach, 2011), we have also found that parents and teachers are good at identifying their students' self-efficacy beliefs, but are much worse at identifying how meaningful their students view school to be. Parents and teachers appear to base their perceptions of how meaningful students find school on how well the students self-regulate their academic behaviors. This seems to support the belief that for many gifted underachievers, self-regulation is a byproduct of the interaction of their self-efficacy, task meaningfulness, and environmental perceptions beliefs. These beliefs are necessary for achievement but may not be the main reason that gifted students are underachieving. With this in mind, it is also important to recognize the significant research that has been conducted in the field of self-regulation (Zimmerman, Bonner, & Kovach, 1996) and acknowledge that time management and study skills are important for achievement. Therefore, I included them as an intervention strategy.

Self-regulation strategies are sometimes clustered into three groups: management strategies, personal standards, and self-monitoring. The categories, however, are not mutually exclusive. Management strategies traditionally cover time management and study skills. Personal standards feature students' risk comfort level, standards for achievement, and perfectionism issues, which were covered in Chapter 5. Self-monitoring includes issues of distractibility, delayed gratification, and performance avoidance. This chapter will review strategies that address many of these issues.

Management strategies generally involve helping students manage their time and implement study skills. Some have described the behavior of many of the underachievers as "swimming in Jello." They appear to know where they want to go, but can't quite organize and execute their activities to achieve their goals (D. Betsy McCoach, personal communication, May 3, 2003).

Premack's Principle

One effective self-discipline strategy is Premack's principle, also commonly known as "Grandma's Rule." The principle is founded on the practice of rewarding one's self with a pleasant task after completing a less pleasant task. The term Grandma's Rule is derived from the practice of rewarding children with dessert for first eating their vegetables.

At the core of many underachievers' self-discipline failure is Premack's principle inversely applied. For example, a parent may, upon arriving home from work, see his daughter watching television and ask her if she has any homework. The girl replies that she has some mathematics homework, but it will not take her long to complete it. The parent suggests she start the homework now. The girl replies that her favorite show is on television, and she will complete her homework as soon as the show is over. The parent responds that she needs to start the homework as soon as the television program is finished. This conversation and similar conversations occur between parents and their children every day. Unfortunately, it is an excellent example of Premack's principle applied inversely. Once the television program is completed, the student has little motivation to do the homework. The parent should have replied, "You better start your homework now, and maybe you will have it finished in time to catch the end of your favorite show." This sends a message that homework is an important task; it also provides a reward system for doing it. Of course, the student might reply that her favorite television show will be over by the time she has finished the mathematics homework. An appropriate parental reply would be, "Next time you will need to remember to have the homework completed before the program begins, or perhaps you can record it and watch it after you have completed your homework." Although this stance may seem harsh to some, not taking it sends the wrong message to the student and reinforces the student's underachieving patterns.

My colleague Joseph Renzulli is one of the most productive and eminent individuals in the field of gifted education. He once shared that writing is not always enjoyable for him, but he enjoys using his exercise machine. Therefore, he will reward himself for writing a given number of pages by allowing himself to use his exercise machine. The parochial school my wife attended required students to wear school uniforms. Her family set a guideline that she could not remove her uniform until she had completed her homework. She would immediately set about completing her homework as soon as she returned home from school so she could change clothes and pursue other activities. That habit transferred to her adult life, and she continues to fervently tackle tasks as soon as they are presented.

Planning for Self-Control

Self-control is widely studied in the social sciences. Self-control strengthens over the lifespan, and it is strongest among older individuals. However, among people of the same age, wide differences in self-control exist. In the Proceedings of the National Academy of Sciences, Moffitt et al. (2011) showed that childhood self-control not only predicted academic performance above and beyond intelligence and social class, it also predicted better decision making that later influenced decisions not to smoke, drop out of high school, or become adolescent parents. Children with higher self-control later became healthier adults, more financially secure, and less likely to have criminal convictions.

Fortunately, Angela Duckworth and her colleagues (Duckworth, Grant, Loew, Oettingen, & Gollwitzer, 2011) have shown that young people can be taught self-regulatory strategies to successfully pursue goals. Self-control involves two actions: starting and staying on track. Starting encompasses recognizing and seizing opportunities to act and overcoming the reluctance to act. The Chinese proverb, "A journey of a thousand miles begins with a single step" certainly rings true. There are several possible reasons why many gifted underachievers simply have trouble starting tasks. Some students may not believe they have the skills to complete the task and are afraid to fail. Fear of failure is a powerful force that paralyzes many people; higher scores on fear of failure measures are associated with procrastination. However, individuals with fear of failure who feel competent do not procrastinate (Pychyl, 2009). Therefore, fearing failure is not debilitating if one has confidence in one's ability. One strategy to address fear of failure is to consider the consequences and missed opportunities of not trying.

Another reason people are also reluctant to start tasks is the issue of perfectionism, which was discussed in Chapter 5. Premack's principle is one option that can be useful to help students start tasks.

After students start a task, the next obstacle is to complete it. Successful self-control involves (a) a commitment to goals that are set and (b) effective planning and enactment of behaviors while striving to achieve those goals. The importance of goal valuation (meaningful learning) certainly comes into play here. Students must be committed to goals in order to have the self-control to achieve them. This is the reason I maintain that much of self-regulation results from positive attitudes about one's ability to perform a task, the importance or meaningfulness of the task, and one's perceptions of environmental support.

Staying on track can be achieved through a three-step process utilizing Gollwitzer's (1999) "if—then—" plan. Once a goal is set, such as completing homework, and the student is committed to achieving that goal, efforts need to be made to stay on track to achieve the goal. The first step is *imagining the positive outcomes associated with completing the goal.* This might include rewards students have been promised if they reach their goal, acceptance into a desired college, or recognition on the honor roll. It might even be as simple as recognition from proud grandparents. Whatever the outcome, it must be achievable, meaningful to the student, and shorter term for young students. The student must buy into the goal and desire the positive outcome associated with it. This first step is essential and may require time to embrace.

Next, students *name critical obstacles that could prevent achieving the desired goal.* In our example, these might include forgetting the homework material at school or not having enough time to do the homework because of a special event scheduled in the evening. The list of critical obstacles can be extensive, and it should be comprehensive. Parents and educators can work with the student to create these, and they are most effective if they are student initiated.

The final step is *developing implementation intentions that result in immediate, effortless, unconscious actions* to overcome the obstacles. These are developed with an "if—then—" statement, based on the critical obstacles, and created *before* students actually encounter these obstacles. For example, assume the family has planned a special dinner outing to celebrate the student's birthday. This could be a possible critical obstacle to completing homework that evening. How can the student overcome that potential obstacle? One possible solution is planning ahead and asking for that day's homework assignment early. Another might be to rise early the next morning and complete the homework before school. The solution is placed in an "if—then—" statement, such as, "If the family has a planned activity that will require most of the evening, then I will ask the teacher for the assignment early and complete it the night before the event." The purpose of this process is for students to anticipate obstacles they might encounter and have a plan that they can automatically fall back on when the obstacles surface. Around 40% of the actions people take are governed by habit rather than actual decisions. The goal of this strategy is to break the unproductive habits underachieving students automatically follow and replace them with habits that enable them to be more productive.

Cognitive Restructuring

The cognitive therapy work of Albert Ellis and Aaron Beck provide the foundation for a useful technique called cognitive restructuring. The technique is based on the assumption that individuals' actions are influenced by what they think. If individuals can change the way they think, they can change their behavior. Habits are not changed instantly, but over time they can change (Strayhorn, 2003).

Although the technique centers around changing attitudes, it is similar to the self-control steps just described and can also be applied to changing behavior. The first step is recognizing whatever attitudes or behaviors are causing the problem or what situation the individual wishes to change. The next step involves prioritizing what attitude or behavior changes need to be made. This is followed by developing a concrete list of positive examples of the needed changes. The individual then practices the newly desired attitudes or behaviors in two ways. One is actual, where the individual encounters real-life situations in which he can implement the desired attitudes or behaviors. The second arena is through fantasy and role-play where the individual imagines having the desired attitudes or behaviors. Finally, the individual recognizes and celebrates successful practice of the desired attitudes or behaviors (Strayhorn, 2003).

Rimm's Study Recommendations

Assuming students have a positive attitude about doing well in school, Sylvia Rimm (2008) offered some helpful tips for managing students' study time:

- Set short term objectives based on long-term goals the student wishes to accomplish.
- Reward activities that are completed.
- Establish a study place in a quiet area away from a television and similar distractions.
- Determine with the student a minimum amount of study time each day, ranging from 20 minutes for a first or second grader to 1 ½ hours for high school students.
- If possible, a same-sex parent should monitor the work.
- Monitor the work until the student internalizes the need to work well.

Monitoring homework is not the same as completing the homework for the student. The main purpose of monitoring the homework is to ensure that it is being completed and completed correctly. The monitoring also signals that parents believe completing homework is important and they value the student completing it. By monitoring the homework, the parent can also assess how the student is performing academically. Does the homework appear to be too easy? Too hard? Is the student frustrated with homework? These observations provide useful information when talking with teachers about the academic progress the student is making. Students should also keep a log of their homework and study activities. Many students believe they are studying much more than they really are. An accurate record of the time spent and activities involved in studying is a useful tool for determining the effectiveness of study time.

Study and Test-Taking Tips

Students differ in the ways they prefer to learn content. Some students enjoy hearing material; others prefer to read it. Although all of us learn through all of our senses, individuals often have preferred methods of learning and studying. Table 2 provides a checklist of preferred ways to study. Based on students' responses, they can plan their studying to maximize its effectiveness.

Many students believe that once they study and take a test, they can move onto other activities. Successful test-taking is much more than simply studying for a test. Being well-prepared for a test involves time management, high-quality note-taking, and regular reviews of material. Reflecting on what study strategies were effective and what study strategies were not effective should be part of students' study strategies. There are three types of reviews that can better prepare students for test-taking: regular, weekly reviews; reviews just before the test; and posttest reviews of the test performance. Doing well on tests involves test anticipation, preparation, and analysis of performance. Table 3 provides an overview of each of these types of reviews.

I was in an airport waiting for a flight when I overheard a father talking on the phone with his son. The father asked how the son had done on his test that day. Following the son's response, the father said, "Did we study the right stuff?" The father had apparently studied with the son, and the son had not performed as well as expected. The father was now trying to determine the reason for the poorer than expected performance. I was impressed with the father's insight. It reflects the posttest suggestions shared in Table 3.

Table 2 Active Study Checklist for Different Learning Styles

RECITE

_____I describe or explain the topic out loud, in my own words.

_____I record into a tape recorder.

_____I teach or explain the information to someone else.

_____I role-play a part.

_____I simulate the lesson.

_____I recite the answers to questions on the topic that I made up myself.

WRITE

_____I make a chapter study review by writing key points on index cards.

_____I make and use flashcards for short-answer questions or concepts.

_____I make lists of related information by categories.

_____I draw a diagram, map, sketch, timeline, or chart from memory, and then I check the book for accuracy.

_____I write questions I think will be on the test and recite the answers.

_____I create semantic maps (visual representation of ideas) to summarize the unit (webs, sequence chains, Venn diagrams).

_____I use mnemonics to remember information.

_____I rewrite class notes, rearranging the information in my own words.

VISUALIZE

_____I close my eyes and picture in my mind what I am trying to remember (chart, map, event, scene, experiment, character).

_____I try to remember where information is located on a page.

_____I picture in my mind how the test will look, based on previous similar tests.

_____I organize and design graphic organizers to put abstract information into concrete and visual form.

_____I represent concepts with symbols so I can remember them.

Note. This list was created by Meredith Greene (2001) for The National Research Center on the Gifted and Talented Improving Academic Achievement Study.

Cornell Notes

Cornell Notes are a simple and easy format for organizing notes to study. Students divide their note-taking paper into three sections (see Figure 5). Students' notes appear in the upper right section. Ideally, students recopy and organize their original notes within one day of making them. This allows them to reflect on what they wrote and possibly clarify confusing entries. Next to their notes on the right, students place possible test questions related to the notes in the upper

Table 3 Three Types of Test-Taking Reviews

Test Anticipation
- What format will the test be? Multiple choice, short answer, essay, combination?
- How much is the test worth?
- How much time will you have to write the test?
- Are you allowed to use notes or text?
- What materials will be needed? Calculator, ruler, pencil?
- Have you regularly reviewed the notes for the test?
- How much study time will you need? When will you study and for how long each time?
- Were previous tests similar to this one? Were there quizzes on this material?

Test Preparation
- Spread your study time over several days and take regular short breaks.
- Study difficult or "boring" subjects first.
- Schedule study time during your best time of day.
- Study where you'll be alert (not in bed or in easy chairs or sofas where you can become too comfortable).
- Revise class and text notes.
- Concentrate on remembering the main ideas and most important information.
- Ask questions of yourself; provide yourself with elaborate explanations.
- Study with a partner to compare notes, and test each other.
- Review main topics and subtopics.

Posttest Analysis
- Did you receive the grade you expected?
- Analyze the missing answers: Were they in your notes? In your text? On a quiz? Did you not provide enough detail?
- Analyze the type of questions: Did you perform better on a certain type of question?
- Did you have enough time to finish the test and to review your answers?

Note. This list was created by Meredith Greene (2001) for The National Research Center on the Gifted and Talented Improving Academic Achievement Study.

left section. For example, if a note on the right provides the number of moons for Saturn, the question on the left might be, "How many moons does Saturn have?" Studying for tests is easy with the combination of the two sections; students cover the right side, read and answer each question, and check their answers by uncovering the appropriate notes on the right. The bottom section is reserved for a summary of the notes written in the student's own words. This section gives the student an opportunity to reflect on the important concepts that are featured in the notes. It also provides an easy summary of

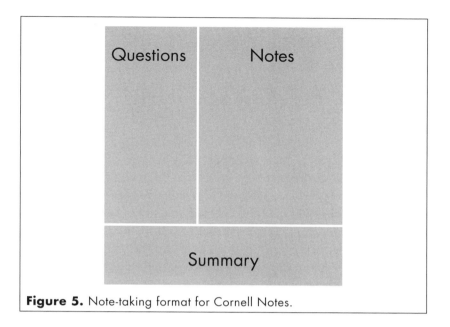

Figure 5. Note-taking format for Cornell Notes.

what content is featured on the note pages. This note-taking format is effective for lecture notes, as well as notes students make of the material they are reading.

Organizing Materials

Teachers and parents can help students organize their work and study time. Greene (2001) recommended that students should create a homework book to record upcoming assignments, projects, tests, and events. They should use a designated two-pocket travel folder in which they label one side as "To Do" and the other as "Done." Keeping all of their important notices and papers in one place saves them time. Students can create reminder checklists, including one called "at school" and one called "at home." Organizing all handouts and papers in chronological order in subject notebooks can be helpful. Students should pack their book bag each night before they go to bed, making sure that they include all of their homework. This makes it easier to later remember forgotten items and eases the morning rush. The book bag should be kept in the same place every night.

Personal Standards

Another aspect of self-regulation involves setting personal standards. Some students may feel that what they are doing is "good enough." If students haven't been academically challenged in the past, they may believe they can achieve satisfactory results with very little effort. Siegle and Reis (1998) reported much weaker relationships between gifted students' perceptions of the effort they put into a subject and their performance in that subject than they reported for their ability in a subject and their performance in the subject.

Gifted students may also underachieve to hide their need for perfection. "The underachiever's perfectionistic goals also undermine her efforts to improve because they focus on the product rather than the process of learning" (Rathvon, 1996, p. 77). Gifted students may be vulnerable because they, more than any other group, approximate perfection to a higher degree, are more often rewarded for it through their accomplishments, and often come to believe perfection is possible. Perfectionistic students often tend to be very black and white about success and achievement. They either want to complete an activity perfectly or they don't want to take part at all. Perfectionism was covered in more depth in Chapter 5.

Students may also have a low-risk comfort level. Perhaps the benefits of achieving don't outweigh the risks, because many students believe that having to work hard means they aren't smart. As discussed earlier, students who view ability as fixed will view challenging tasks as tests of their intelligence. These students' reticence to achieve may be a defense mechanism to maintain their "gifted status." Conversely, students who believe that intelligence is malleable and can be developed will view challenging tasks as opportunities for improvement (Dweck, 1975).

Students with a performance orientation, which was described in Chapter 4, may demonstrate performance avoidance. Such students are motivated by generous reinforcement for success. They respond better to assignments that have detailed instructions with specific grading criteria. When working with performance avoidance students, teachers should provide detailed assignment instructions and include an evaluation rubric when appropriate. They should divide larger tasks into smaller tasks and recognize the student's performance at each step. These students may also respond positively if their desks are near the teacher's desk.

Ensure Students Need Study Skills

Many gifted students may lack self-management strategies such as time management and study skills. Because gifted students often progress through the early years of school without being challenged, they sometimes fail to develop the self-management skills that other students master. In the early grades, good memory and fast processing skills can compensate for note-taking and other study skills. Often, educators attempt to teach students study skills before students need those skills to be successful. This process usually frustrates both the teachers and the students. Self-regulatory skills are more likely to be internalized when they are needed to solve the problem at hand. A solution to the problem is to provide gifted students with an academically challenging curriculum and intellectual stimulation early and throughout their school careers so that students have opportunities to develop self-management skills (Siegle & McCoach, 2005b).

chapter 12

Putting It All Together

> *The future belongs to those who believe in the beauty of their dreams.*
>
> —Eleanor Roosevelt

My work and interest in gifted students spans three decades. Like many educators, I stumbled into the field, fell in love with it, and have remained passionate about developing students' interests and talents. Now, as a father later in life with two small children, my interest has become more personal. As a gifted and talented coordinator in Montana, I encountered motivated and achieving students, as well as those who could do better but were not. This began a journey that ultimately led to earning a Ph.D. and spending most of my academic life thinking about and studying gifted underachievement. As my wife and I raise our two young children, we are very cognizant of our role in helping them develop an achievement orientation attitude. Having two parents with advanced degrees in gifted education can lead to relentless reflections and discussions on parenting. We count ourselves lucky to have Sylvia Rimm as a surrogate grandparent and Joe Renzulli and Sally Reis as a surrogate uncle and aunt. We take every opportunity to help our young children recognize their accomplishments and the important role their effort plays in their progress.

Our young daughter recently commented that she did not like one of her preschool teachers as well as the other because she gave her "hard things to do." We capitalized on the moment to share how "doing hard things helps us become better" and how lucky she was that Miss Amanda was taking the time to help her become better at writing. We are thankful that this dedicated educator recognized our daughter's advanced skills and was not content to let her learning languish while she paralleled her peers' activities. Taking the difficult path is a not a natural tendency. Parents are extremely important models in helping their children recognize the important role hard work plays in developing one's skills and feeling fulfilled. As parents, we need to embrace challenges in our own lives and share those experiences with our children. We need to share the satisfaction that comes from hard work and a job well done. We need to model curiosity, wonder in the world around us, and a love of learning. In effect, we need to reflect and encourage the natural love of learning that our children display while modeling the important role that applied effort plays in achievements.

In the classic Tennessee Williams play, *The Glass Menagerie,* Laura asked her mother for what she should wish, and Amanda responded, "Happiness . . . and just a little bit of good fortune." At the core, happiness is what parents wish for their children.

Thomas Kehle, a colleague at The University of Connecticut, has researched what makes people happy (Kehle & Bray, 2004). Although we may expect the response would be "lots of money," Kehle has found four interactive factors affect happiness. In his *RICH* (*R*esources, *I*ntimacy, *C*ompetence, and *H*ealth) Theory, he proposes that improvement in any one component of the theory results in improvement of the others.

Happy people have resources. They are not necessarily rich, but they have resources to ensure individual freedom and self-determination. Happy people have intimacy. Intimacy is defined as one or more significant personal relationships. It involves empathy and the appreciation and enjoyment of a friend's company. Happy people feel competent compared to some standard. They do not need to feel competent about everything, but they do feel competent in something. Competence is attributed to one's own abilities. Finally, happy people tend to have mental and physical health.

When each of these four elements is present, people tend to be happy. Parents and educators can use this model to help promote children's happiness and achievement. They can provide young people with time and independence to explore their interests and talents. They can support friendships with same-age peers and intellectual peers. They can help young people recognize and appreciate their talents. Finally, they can encourage a healthy lifestyle that includes some physical activity and minimizes undue stressors.

In 1983, E. Paul Torrance published his *Manifesto for Children*, a guide for leading a creative life. In recognition of Dr. Torrance's concern for young people and his passion for their talent development, I began my term as NAGC president several years ago by proposing the Gifted Children's Bill of Rights (Siegle, 2007). Although many of the 10 rights listed in the Bill pertain to all children, they are particularly relevant for students with special gifts and talents. Promoting these rights stimulates talent development and avoids some of the conditions often associated with underachievement.

Gifted Children's Bill of Rights

Gifted Children Have a Right to Know About Their Giftedness

Children need to understand that giftedness is not something that was bestowed upon them. Although it is true that gifted students often acquire skills more quickly and easily than their peers, gifted children do learn these skills over time. It is important for gifted children to recognize that the talents they possess are acquired, they had something to do with acquiring them, and they are capable of further developing these talents and even acquiring new ones. They need to learn to take responsibility for developing their gifts. They need to understand that having to work hard does not mean they are not gifted and that working hard can even make them more gifted.

Gifted Children Have a Right to Learn Something New Every Day

Gifted children, like all children, have the right to learn something new every day; they also have the right to learn something new in school every day. Unfortunately, this is not always the case. Karen Westberg and her colleagues (1993) found that gifted children spend up to 80% of their time in classrooms doing exactly what everyone else is doing. For students who are academically advanced, this results in a tremendous loss of learning opportunities. When most of their school day is spent on material they already know or material they could learn more quickly, gifted children are in danger of never reaching their potential. They do not experience the challenges that are required to reach high levels of productivity in their talent areas.

Gifted Children Have a Right to Be Passionate About Their Talent Area Without Apologies

Successful people are passionate about what they do. Gifted children often exhibit a single fascination with a topic or talent area and devote endless hours to learning about or perfecting it. Such dedication is needed to develop expertise in an area. Although a minimal level of knowledge about a variety of topics in life is useful, children who show a strong interest in an area should be encouraged to pursue that interest.

Gifted Children Have a Right to Have an Identity Beyond Their Talent Area

Young people are works in progress. Their interests and identities develop and change. In the early years and during adolescence, they are not only developing their talents, they are also developing their sense of self. They need to understand that their value as a human being and the esteem with which parents hold them go beyond the exceptional talents they possess. It is easy for parents to focus on developing their children's talents and to forget to recognize the many other fine traits their children possess. Children need to understand that, although their parents value their gifts, love is unconditional, and they will be loved regardless of how well they perform in their talent area or the mistakes they might make.

Gifted Children Have a Right to Feel Good About Their Accomplishments

Although children's identities go beyond their giftedness, they do have a right to take pride in doing something well that required effort. Individuals should be neither boastful nor ashamed of things beyond their control such as their height or a physical challenges; however, they do have the right to feel good about accomplishments they did control. Children should feel good about performing well and the effort and dedication that were necessary to excel. Having a sense of pride in one's accomplishments is healthy as long as it does not belittle the efforts and accomplishments of others.

Gifted Children Have a Right to Make Mistakes

Perfectionism can be a problem for gifted children, and taking healthy risks is an important part of developing talents. Thomas J. Watson, the man who built IBM into an international success, said, "If you want to succeed, double your failure rate." Mistakes are part of the learning process, and gifted individuals experience a variety of successes and failures as they strive for excellence. Parents can help their children understand that making mistakes is a natural part of learning and that successful individuals study and learn from their mistakes.

Gifted Children Have a Right to Seek Guidance in the Development of Their Talent

Talent does not flourish in isolation. It needs to be assisted and nurtured by those with advanced skills and experience. This can require the assistance of expertise outside traditional education venues. Isaac Newton wrote in a letter to fellow English scientist Robert Hooke, "If I have seen further, it is by standing on the shoulders of giants." Gifted children need giants to guide them, and this may require mentors who share their passion and talents. The well-known educational psychologist Benjamin Bloom (1985) noted that there is no shortage of talent, just a shortage of resources to develop it. Gifted children will need assistance in finding the resources necessary to guide their talent development.

Gifted Children Have a Right to Have Multiple Peer Groups and a Variety of Friends

Gifted children may have trouble finding same-age peers who share their interests and passions. They may be interested in social issues at an earlier age than their age-mates and may also have trouble finding same-age peers with similar abilities. For these reasons, gifted children may have a variety of peer groups, some based on a similar age, others based on interest or intellectual development. It is not uncommon for gifted children to have younger and older friends and friends in different arenas. They may also choose not to have very many friends. A few close relationships may be sufficient.

Gifted Children Have a Right to Choose Which of Their Talent Areas They Wish to Pursue

Some gifted children excel in a variety of different areas; this is called multipotentiality. Although this may not seem problematic, these children can experience difficulty selecting a major when entering college or a career path upon graduation. Just as gifted children have the right to pursue those talent areas that interest them, they also have a right not to pursue every area in which they excel. High levels of performance require sustained effort over time. Few individuals are able to achieve this in multiple talent areas. Gifted children may exhibit interests in a variety of areas and derive great pleasure from participating in them, but the time and effort necessary to develop high levels of expertise usually necessitates focusing in one area.

Gifted Children Have a Right Not to Be Gifted at Everything

Many gifted children may excel in one area but be average, or even below average, in another area. Young children in particular can show such asynchronous development when their physical skills and emotional maturity do not match their intellectual maturity. Gifted students with perfectionism issues may have trouble accepting that they do not do everything well and may avoid activities in which they do not excel. Parents can encourage their children to experience a variety of activities without feeling pressure to excel at all of them. On the other hand, there is no reason to force gifted children to expend considerable amounts of time and effort pursuing hobbies in which they are neither interested nor talented in the hopes of creating well-rounded children. This can be frustrating to both parents and their gifted children. Albert Einstein's passion for mathematics and physics certainly overshadowed his skills in other areas, but those areas in which he did not excel were insignificant compared to what he accomplished in his chosen field.

By encouraging young people to recognize and develop their talents, we move humanity forward. This is important for two reasons. First, the nation and the world will benefit from what gifted individuals accomplish. Second, and perhaps more importantly, even if these individuals do not become accomplished scientists or best-selling authors, they lead happier and more enriched lives when they are allowed to pursue their interests and develop their talents. It is important not to give up when students are not performing at expected levels. Some students naturally turn low achievement around with maturation. Others blossom when they finally have a chance to fully pursue a passion area. Some students reverse their underachievement as the result of a caring teacher or significant mentor whereas some reverse underachievement when they move to a healthier environment. Different types of underachievers require different combinations of counseling and instructional or curricular modifications. Successful interventions incorporate both proactive and preventative counseling and innovative instructional interventions. All of us, like students who underachieve, are works in progress that need support and nurturance to achieve our potential. By helping students recognize that they have the skills to do to well, by making their learning experiences meaningful, and by providing a supportive environment, we move students toward appreciating their gifts and talents and fulfilling their potential. As frustrating as underachievement is to parents and teachers, ultimately, it is the student who must be willing to change behaviors. As Whitmore (1986) noted more than a quarter of a century ago, "The final choice, obviously, is the child's; he or she must want to change and believe effort will be rewarded by sufficient success and personal satisfaction" (p. 69).

References

Achter, J. A., Lubinski, D., & Benbow, C. P. (1996). Multipotentiality among the intellectually gifted: "It was never there and already it's vanishing." *Journal of Counseling Psychology, 43*, 65–76.

Adderholdt, M., & Goldberg, J. (1999). *Perfectionism: What's bad about being too good?* Minneapolis, MN: Free Spirit.

Adderholdt-Elliot, M. (1987). *Perfectionism: What's bad about being too good?* Minneapolis, MN: Free Spirit.

Adelson, J. L., & Wilson, H. E. (2009). *Letting go of perfect: Overcoming perfectionism in kids.* Waco, TX: Prufrock Press.

Albaili, M. A. (2003). Motivational goal orientations of intellectually gifted achieving and underachieving students in the United Arab Emirates. *Social Behavior and Personality, 31,* 107–120.

Alberta Education. (2006). *Focusing on success: Teaching students with Attention Deficit/Hyperactivity Disorder, grades 1–12.* Retrieved from http://education.alberta.ca/media/513151/e_chap4.pdf

Alter, A. L., Aronson, J. M., Darley, J. M., Rodriguez, C., & Ruble, D. N. (2010). Rising to the threat: Reducing stereotype threat by reframing the threat as a challenge. *Journal of Experimental Social Psychology, 46,* 166–171.

Ames, C. A. (1990). Motivation: What teachers need to know. *Teachers College Record, 91,* 409–421.

Antony, M. W., & Swinson, R. P. (1998). *When perfect isn't good enough: Strategies for coping with perfectionism.* Oakland, CA: New Harbinger Publications.

Archambault, F. A., Jr., Westberg, K. L., Brown, S. W., Hallmark, B. W., Emmons, C. L., & Zhang, W. (1993). *Regular classroom practices with gifted students: Results of a national survey of classroom teachers* (Research Monograph 93102). Storrs: University of Connecticut, The National Research Center on the Gifted and Talented.

Aronson, J., & Juarez, L. (2012). Growth mindsets in the laboratory and the real world. In R. F. Subotnik, A. Robinson, C. M. Callahan, & E. J. Gubbins (Eds.), *Malleable minds: Translating insights from psychology and neuroscience to gifted education* (pp. 19–36). Storrs: University of Connecticut, The National Research Center on the Gifted and Talented.

Assouline, S. G., Colangelo, N., Ihrig, D., & Forstadt, L. (2006). Attributional choices for academic success and failure by intellectually gifted students. *Gifted Child Quarterly, 50,* 283–294.

Baker, J. A., Bridger, R., & Evans, K. (1998). Models of underachievement among gifted preadolescents: The role of personal, family, and school factors. *Gifted Child Quarterly, 42,* 5–14.

Bandura, A. (1977). Self-efficacy: Toward a unifying theory of behavioral change. *Psychological Review, 84,* 191–215.

Bandura, A. (1982). Self-efficacy mechanism in human agency. *American Psychologist, 37,* 122–147.

Bandura, A. (1986). *Social foundations of thought and action: A social cognition theory.* Englewood Cliffs, NJ: Prentice-Hall.

Bandura, A. (1993). Perceived self-efficacy in cognitive development and functioning. *Educational Psychologist, 28,* 117–148.

Baslanti, U., & McCoach, D. B. (2006). Gifted underachievers and factors affecting underachievement. *Roeper Review, 28,* 210–215.

Baum, S. M., Renzulli, J. S., & Hébert, T. P. (1995). Reversing under-achievement: Creative productivity as a systematic intervention. *Gifted Child Quarterly, 39,* 224–235.

Begin, J., & Gagné, F. (1994a). Predictors of attitudes toward gifted education: A review of the literature and blueprints for future research. *Journal for the Education of the Gifted, 17,* 161–179.

Begin, J., & Gagné, F. (1994b). Predictors of a general attitude toward gifted education. *Journal for the Education of the Gifted, 17,* 74–86.

Berndt, T. J. (1999). Friends' influence on students' adjustment to school. *Educational Psychologist, 34,* 15–28.

Birth Order Plus. (n.d.). *Intro to birth order.* Retrieved from http://www.birthorderplus.com/birthorder/intro.htm

Bloom, B. J. (Ed.). (1985). *Developing talent in young people.* New York, NY: Ballantine.

Brophy, J. (1998). *Motivating students to learn.* Boston, MA: McGraw-Hill.

Brophy, J. (2008). Developing students' appreciation for what is taught in school. *Educational Psychologist, 43,* 132–141.

Brown, B. B., Mounts, N., Lamborn, S. D., & Steinberg, L. (1993). Parenting practices and peer group affiliation in adolescence. *Child Development, 64,* 467–482.

Burns, K. C., & Isbell, L. M. (2007). Promoting malleability is not one size fits all: Priming implicit theories of intelligence as a function of self-theories. *Self and Identity, 6,* 51–63.

Buschkuehl, M., Jaeggi, S. M., Shah, P., & Jonides, J. (2012). Working memory training and transfer. In R. F. Subotnik, A. Robinson, C. M. Callahan, & E. J. Gubbins (Eds.), *Malleable minds: Translating insights from psychology and neuroscience to gifted education* (pp. 101–115). Storrs: University of Connecticut, The National Research Center on the Gifted and Talented.

Campbell, J. R., & Verna, M. A. (2007). Effective parental influences: Academic home climate linked to children's achievement. *Educational Research and Evaluation, 13,* 501–519.

Carr, M., Borkowski, J. G., & Maxwell, S. E. (1991). Motivational components of underachievement. *Developmental Psychology, 27,* 108–118.

Chan, L. K. S. (1996). Motivational orientations and metacognitive abilities of intellectually gifted students. *Gifted Child Quarterly, 40*, 184–193.

Chen, X. (1997, June). *Students' peer groups in high school: The pattern and relationship to educational outcomes* (NCES 97-055). Washington, DC: U.S. Department of Education.

Clasen, D. R., & Clasen, R. E. (1995). Underachievement of highly able students and the peer society. *Gifted and Talented International, 10*(2), 67–75.

Cohen, G. L., Garcia, J., Apfel, N., & Master, A. (2006). Reducing the racial achievement gap: A social-psychological intervention. *Science, 313*, 1307–1310.

Colangelo, N. (2003). Counseling gifted students. In N. Colangelo & G. A. Davis (Eds.), *Handbook of gifted education* (pp. 373–387). Boston, MA: Allyn & Bacon.

Colangelo, N., Kerr, B., Christensen, P., & Maxey, J. (1993). A comparison of gifted underachievers and gifted high achievers. *Gifted Child Quarterly, 37*, 155–160.

Cole, N. S. (1997). *The ETS gender study: How males and females perform in educational settings.* Princeton, NJ: Educational Testing Service.

Coleman, L. J., & Cross, T. L. (2005). *Being gifted in school: An introduction to development, guidance, and teaching* (2nd ed.). Waco, TX: Prufrock Press.

Collins, J. L. (1984). *Self-efficacy and ability in achievement behavior* (Unpublished doctoral dissertation). Stanford University, Stanford, CA.

Colvin, G. (2008). *Talent is overrated: What really separates world-class performers from everybody else.* New York, NY: Penguin.

Conger, D., & Long, M. (2010). Why are men falling behind? Gender gaps in college performance and persistence. *Annals of the American Academy of Political and Social Science, 627*, 184–214.

Cramond, B., & Martin, C. E. (1987). Inservice and preservice teachers' attitudes toward the academically brilliant. *Gifted Child Quarterly, 31*, 15–19.

Csikszentmihalyi, M. (1993). *The evolving self: A psychology for the third millennium.* New York, NY: Harper Perennial.

Dai, D. Y. (2010). *The nature and nurture of giftedness: A new framework for understanding gifted education.* New York, NY: Teachers College Press.

Davis, G. A., Rimm, S. B., & Siegle, D. (2011). *Education of the gifted and talented* (6th ed.). Boston, MA: Pearson.

Deary, J., Strand, S., Smith, P., & Fernandes, C. (2007). Intelligence and educational achievement. *Intelligence, 35,* 13–21.

Deci, E. L., & Ryan, R. M. (1985). *Intrinsic motivation and self-determination in human behavior.* New York, NY: Plenum.

Delisle, J., & Galbraith, J. (2002). *When gifted kids don't have all the answers: How to meet their social and emotional needs.* Minneapolis, MN: Free Spirit.

Diamond, A. (2012). How I came full circle from the social end of psychology, to neuroscience, and back again in an effort to understand the development of cognitive control. In R. F. Subotnik, A. Robinson, C. M. Callahan, & E. J. Gubbins (Eds.), *Malleable minds: Translating insights from psychology and neuroscience to gifted education* (pp. 55–83). Storrs: University of Connecticut, The National Research Center on the Gifted and Talented.

Dixon, F. A., Lapsley, D. K., & Hanchon, T. A. (2004). An empirical typology of perfectionism in gifted adolescents. *Gifted Child Quarterly, 48,* 95–106.

Dowdall, C. B., & Colangelo, N. (1982). Underachieving gifted students: Review and implications. *Gifted Child Quarterly, 26,* 179–184.

Duckworth, A. L., Grant, H., Loew, B., Oettingen, G., & Gollwitzer, P. M. (2011). Self-regulation strategies improve self-discipline in adolescents: Benefits of mental contrasting and implementation intentions. *Educational Psychology, 31,* 17–26.

Duckworth, A. L., & Seligman, M. E. P. (2006). Self-discipline outdoes IQ in predicting academic performance of adolescents. *Psychological Science, 16,* 939–944.

Dweck, C. S. (1975). The role of expectations and attributions in the alleviation of learned helplessness. *Journal of Personality and Social Psychology, 31*, 674–685.

Dweck, C. S. (1999). *Self-theories: Their role in motivation, personality, and development.* Philadelphia, PA: Psychology Press.

Dweck, C. S. (2012). Mindsets and malleable minds: Implications for giftedness and talent. In R. F. Subotnik, A. Robinson, C. M. Callahan, & E. J. Gubbins (Eds.), *Malleable minds: Translating insights from psychology and neuroscience to gifted education* (pp. 7–18). Storrs: University of Connecticut, The National Research Center on the Gifted and Talented.

Dweck, C. S., & Molden, D. C. (2005). Self-theories: Their impact on competence motivation and acquisition. In A. J. Elliot & C. S. Dweck (Eds.), *Handbook of competence and motivation* (pp. 122–140). New York, NY: The Guilford Press.

Eccles, J. S., & Wigfield, A. (1995). In the mind of the actor: The structure of adolescents' achievement task values and expectancy-related beliefs. *Personality and Social Psychology Bulletin, 21*, 215–225.

Emerick, L. J. (1988). *Academic underachievement among the gifted: Students' perceptions of factors relating to the reversal of the academic underachievement pattern* (Unpublished doctoral dissertation). University of Connecticut, Storrs.

Emerick, L. J. (1992). Academic underachievement among the gifted: Students' perceptions of factors that reverse the pattern. *Gifted Child Quarterly, 36*, 140–146.

Ericsson, K. A., Krampe, R. T., & Tesch-Römer, C. (1993). The role of deliberate practice in the acquisition of expert performance. *Psychological Review, 100*, 363–406.

Ericsson, K. A., Prietula, M. J., & Cokely, E. T. (2007). The making of an expert. *Harvard Business Review.* Retrieved from http://www.coachingmanagement.nl/The%20Making%20of%20an%20Expert.pdf

Fine, M. J., & Pitts, R. (1980). Intervention with underachieving gifted children: Rationale and strategies. *Gifted Child Quarterly, 24*, 51–55.

Ford, D. Y. (1996). *Reversing underachievement among gifted Black students*. New York, NY: Teachers College Press.

Fredricks, J. A., Alfeld, C., & Eccles, J. (2010). Developing and fostering passion in academic and nonacademic domains. *Gifted Child Quarterly, 54,* 18–30.

Freedman, J. (2000). *Personal and school factors influencing academic success or underachievement of intellectually gifted students in middle childhood* (Unpublished doctoral dissertation). Yale University, New Haven, CT.

Frost, R. O., Marten, P., Lahart, C., & Rosenblate, R. (1990). The dimensions of perfectionism. *Cognitive Therapy and Research, 14,* 449–468.

Gagné, F. (2005). From gifts to talents: The DMGT as a developmental model. In R. J. Sternberg & J. E. Davidson (Eds.), *Conceptions of giftedness* (2nd ed., pp. 98–119). New York, NY: Cambridge University Press.

Gallagher, J., Harradine, C. C., & Coleman, M. R. (1997). Challenge or boredom? Gifted students' views on their schooling. *Roeper Review, 19,* 132–136.

Gallagher, J. J. (1994). Current and historical thinking on education for gifted and talented students. In P. O'Connell-Ross (Ed.), *National excellence: A case for developing America's talent: An anthology of readings* (pp. 83–107). Washington, DC: Office of Educational Research and Improvement.

Gardner, H. (1985). *Frames of mind: The theory of multiple intelligences.* New York, NY: Basic Books.

Garn, A. C., Matthews, M. S., & Jolly, J. L. (2010). Parental influences on the academic motivation of gifted students: A self-determination theory perspective. *Gifted Child Quarterly, 54,* 263–272.

Gentry, M., Rizza, M. G., & Gable, R. K. (2001). Gifted students' perceptions of their class activities: Differences among rural, urban, and suburban student attitudes. *Gifted Child Quarterly, 45,* 115–129.

Gollwitzer, P. M. (1999). Implementation intentions: Strong effects of simple plans. *American Psychologist, 54,* 493–503.

Good, T. L., & Brophy, J. E. (1994). *Looking in classrooms* (6th ed.). New York, NY: HarperCollins.

Gorrell, J., & Trentham, L. (1992). Teachers' preferred modes of helping students. *Journal of Research and Development in Education, 25,* 142–148.

Gowan, J. (1955). The underachieving gifted child—A problem for everyone. *Exceptional Children, 21,* 247–271.

Graham, S., & Barker, G. P. (1990). The down side of help: An attribution-developmental analysis of helping behavior as a low-ability cue. *Journal of Educational Psychology, 82,* 7–14.

Grant, H., & Dweck, C. S. (2003). Clarifying achievement goals and their impact. *Journal of Personality and Social Psychology, 85,* 541–553.

Green, K., Fine, M. J., & Tollefson, N. (1988). Family systems characteristics and underachieving gifted males. *Gifted Child Quarterly, 32,* 267–272.

Greene, M. (2001). *Environmental perceptions.* Retrieved from http://www.gifted.uconn.edu/siegle/SchoolPerceptions/INDEX.HTM

Greenspon, T. S. (2002). *Freeing our families from perfectionism.* Minneapolis, MN: Free Spirit.

Greenspon, T. S. (2006, Spring). Getting beyond perfectionism. *Gifted Education Communicator, 30*–33.

Greenspon, T. S. (2012). Perfectionism: A counselor's role in a recovery process. In T. L. Cross & J. R. Cross (Eds.), *Handbook for counselors serving students with gifts and talents: Development, relationships, school issues, and counseling needs/interventions* (pp. 597–613). Waco, TX: Prufrock Press.

Greenspon, T. S., Parker, W. D., & Schuler, P. A. (2000). The authors' dialogue. *Journal of Secondary Gifted Education, 11,* 209–214.

Heacox, D. (1991). *Up from underachievement.* Minneapolis, MN: Free Spirit.

Hébert, T. P. (2011). *Understanding the social and emotional lives of gifted students.* Waco, TX: Prufrock Press.

Hébert, T. P., & Olenchak, F. R. (2000). Mentors for gifted underachieving males: Developing potential and realizing promise. *Gifted Child Quarterly, 44,* 196–207.

Heller, K. A., & Ziegler, A. (1996). Gender differences in mathematics and the sciences: Can attributional retraining improve the performance of gifted females? *Gifted Child Quarterly, 40,* 200–210.

Heller, K. A., & Ziegler, A. (2001). Attributional retraining: A classroom-integrated model for nurturing talents in mathematics and the sciences. In N. Colangelo & S. Assouline (Eds.), *Talent development IV* (pp. 205–217). Scottsdale, AZ: Great Potential Press.

Hewitt, P., & Flett, G. (1991). Perfectionism in the self and social contexts: Conceptualization, assessment, and association with psychopathology. *Journal of Personality and Social Psychology, 60,* 456–470.

Hunsaker, S. L. (Ed.). (2012). *Identification: The theory and practice of identifying students for gifted and talented education services.* Mansfield Center, CT: Creative Learning Press.

Hynes, A. M., & Hynes-Berry, M. (1994). *Biblio-poetry therapy, the interactive process: A handbook.* St. Cloud, MN: North Star Press of St. Cloud.

Johnsen, S. K. (Ed.). (2011). *Identifying gifted students: A practical guide* (2nd ed.). Waco, TX: Prufrock Press.

Kanevsky, L., & Keighley, T. (2003). To produce or not to produce? Understanding boredom and the honor in underachievement. *Roeper Review, 26,* 20–28.

Kaplan, S. (2006, July). *Gifted students in a contemporary society: Implications for curriculum.* Keynote at the 29th annual University of Connecticut Confratute, Storrs, CT.

Kehle, T. J., & Bray, M. A. (2004). RICH theory: The promotion of happiness. *Psychology in the Schools, 41,* 43–49.

Kehle, T. J., & Bray, M. A. (2011). Individual differences. In M. A. Bray & T. J. Kehle (Eds.), *The Oxford handbook of school psychology* (pp. 63–78). Oxford, England: Oxford University Press.

Kindermann, T. A. (1993). Natural peer groups as contexts for individual development: The case of children's motivation in school. *Developmental Psychology, 29,* 970–977.

Krouse, J. H., & Krouse, H. J. (1981). Toward a multimodal theory of underachievement. *Educational Psychologist, 16,* 151–164.

Lacasse, M. A. (1999). *Personality types among gifted underachieving adolescents: A comparison with gifted achievers and non-gifted underachievers* (Unpublished doctoral dissertation). York University, Toronto, CA.

Ladner, M., & Hammons, C. (2001). Special but unequal: Race and special education. In C. E. Finn, A. J. Rotherham, & C. R. Hokanso (Eds.), *Rethinking special education for a new century* (pp. 85–110). Washington, DC: Thomas B. Fordham.

Long-Mitchell, L. A. (2011). High-achieving Black adolescents' perceptions of how teachers impact their academic achievement. In J. A. Castellano & A. D. Frazier (Eds.), *Special populations in gifted education: Understanding our most able students from diverse backgrounds* (pp. 99–123). Waco, TX: Prufrock Press.

Luscombe, B. (2010, September 1). Workplace salaries: At last, women on top. *Time*. Retrieved from http://www.time.com/time/business/articles/0,8599,2015274,00.html

Lyman, R. D., Prentice-Dunn, S., Wilson, D. R., & Bonfilio, S. A. (1984). The effect of success or failure on self-efficacy and task persistence of conduct-disordered children. *Psychology in the Schools, 21*, 516–519.

Mallinger, A. E., & DeWyze, J. (1992). *Too perfect: When being in control gets out of control.* New York, NY: Random House.

Mandel, H. P., & Marcus, S. I. (1988). *The psychology of underachievement.* New York, NY: Wiley & Sons.

Mandel, H. P., & Marcus, S. I. (1995). *Could do better.* New York, NY: Wiley & Sons.

Martin, A. J., & Marsh, H. W. (2006). Academic resilience and its psychological and educational correlates: A construct validity approach. *Psychology in the Schools, 43*, 267–281.

Marzano, R. J. (2000). *Transforming classroom grading.* Alexandria, VA: Association for Supervision and Curriculum Development.

Matthews, M. S., & McBee, M. T. (2007). School factors and the underachievement of gifted students in a talent search summer program. *Gifted Child Quarterly, 51*, 167–181.

McCall, R. B. (1994). Academic underachievers. *Current Directions in Psychological Science, 3*, 15–19.

McCall, R. B., Evahn, C., & Kratzer, L. (1992). *High school under-achievers: What do they achieve as adults?* Newbury Park, CA: SAGE.

McCoach, D. B. (2002). A validity study of the School Attitude Assessment Survey (SAAS). *Measurement and Evaluation in Counseling and Development, 35,* 66–77.

McCoach, D. B., & Siegle, D. (1999, November). *Academic challenge: Are we barking up the wrong tree?* Paper presented at the 46th annual convention of the National Association for Gifted Children, Albuquerque, NM.

McCoach, D. B., & Siegle, D. (2001). A comparison of high achievers' and low achievers' attitudes, perceptions, and motivations. *Academic Exchange Quarterly, 5*(2), 71–76.

McCoach, D. B., & Siegle, D. (2003a). Factors that differentiate underachieving gifted students from high-achieving gifted students. *Gifted Child Quarterly, 47,* 144–154.

McCoach, D. B., & Siegle, D. (2003b). The structure and function of academic self-concept in gifted and general education samples. *Roeper Review, 25,* 61–65.

McCoach, D. B., & Siegle, D. (2007). What predicts teachers' attitudes toward the gifted? *Gifted Child Quarterly, 51,* 246–255.

McNabb, T. (2003). Motivational issues: Potential to performance. In N. Colangelo & G. A. Davis (Eds.), *Handbook of gifted education* (3rd ed., pp. 417–423). Boston, MA: Allyn & Bacon.

Michener, L. (1980). A survey of the attitudes of administrators, teachers, and community members toward the education of gifted children and youth. *Dissertation Abstracts International, 41,* 4678A-4679A (University Microfilm No. 81-09, 558).

Moffitt, T. E., Arseneault, L., Belsky, D., Dickson, N., Hancox, R., Harrington, H., . . . Caspi, A. (2011). A gradient of childhood self-control predicts health, wealth, and public safety. *Proceedings of the National Academy of Sciences, 108,* 2693–2698.

Moon, S. M., & Hall, A. S. (1998). Family therapy with intellectually and creatively gifted children. *Journal of Marital and Family Therapy, 24,* 59–80.

Mueller, C. M., & Dweck, C. S. (1998). Intelligence praise can undermine motivation and performance. *Journal of Personality and Social Psychology, 75,* 33–52.

Multon, K. D., Brown, S. D., & Lent, R. W. (1991). Relation of self-efficacy beliefs to academic outcomes: A meta-analytic investigation. *Journal of Counseling Psychology, 38,* 30–38.

Murphy, M. C., & Dweck, C. S. (2010). A culture of genius: How an organization's lay theory shapes people's cognition, affect, and behavior. *Personality and Social Psychology Bulletin, 36,* 283–296.

Murphy, P. K., & Alexander, P. A. (2001). A motivated exploration of motivation terminology. *Contemporary Educational Psychology, 25,* 3–53.

National Association for Gifted Children. (2010). *Redefining giftedness for a new century: Shifting the paradigm.* Retrieved from http://www.nagc.org/index.aspx?id=6404

Ogbu, J. U. (1978). *Minority education and caste.* New York, NY: Academic Press.

Olszewski-Kubilius, P., & Lee, S.-Y. (2011). Gender and other group differences in performance on off-level tests: Changes in the 21st century. *Gifted Child Quarterly, 55,* 54–73.

Owen, S. V. (1989, October). *Building self-efficacy instruments.* Paper presented at the 17th annual Nursing Research Conference on Instrumentation in Nursing, Tucson, AZ.

Pakulak, E., & Neville, H. (2012). Interacting experiential and genetic effects on human neurocognitive development. In R. F. Subotnik, A. Robinson, C. M. Callahan, & E. J. Gubbins (Eds.), *Malleable minds: Translating insights from psychology and neuroscience to gifted education* (pp. 85–99). Storrs: University of Connecticut, The National Research Center on the Gifted and Talented.

Parker, W. D., & Mills, C. J. (1996). The incidence of perfectionism in gifted students. *Gifted Child Quarterly, 40,* 194–199.

Pehrsson, D.-E., & McMillen, P. (2007). Bibliotherapy: Overview and implications for counselors. *Professional Counseling Digest.* Retrieved from http://counselingoutfitters.com/vistas/ACAPCD/ACAPCD-02.pdf

Pendarvis, E. D., Howley, A. A., & Howley C. B. (1990). *The abilities of gifted children.* Englewood Cliffs, NJ: Prentice Hall.

Peterson, J. S. (2001). Successful adults who were once adolescent underachievers. *Gifted Child Quarterly, 45,* 236–250.

Peterson, J. S., & Colangelo, N. (1996). Gifted achievers and underachievers: A comparison of patterns found in school files. *Journal of Counseling and Development, 74,* 399–406.

Pickering, M. (1986). Communication. *EXPLORATIONS, A Journal of Research of the University of Maine, 3*(1), 16–19.

Plucker, J., Burroughs, N., & Song, R. (2010). *Mind the (other) gap! The growing excellence gap in K–12 education.* Bloomington, IN: CEEP.

Plucker, J. A., & McIntire, J. (1996). Academic survivability in high-potential, middle school students. *Gifted Child Quarterly, 40,* 7–14.

Poropat, A. E. (2009). A meta-analysis of the five-factor model of personality and academic performance. *Psychological Bulletin, 135,* 322–338.

Porter, L. (2005). *Gifted young children: A guide for teachers and parents* (2nd ed.). New York, NY: Open University Press.

Price, J. (2011, September 28). *The perfect is the enemy of the good.* Retrieved from http://maglinty.blogspot.com/2011/09/perfect-is-enemy-of-good.html

Purcell, J. H. (1994). *The status of programs for high ability students.* (Research Monograph CRS94306). Storrs: University of Connecticut, The National Research Center on the Gifted and Talented.

Pychyl, T. A. (2009). Don't delay: Understanding procrastination and how to achieve our goals. *Psychology Today.* Retrieved from http://www.psychologytoday.com/blog/dont-delay/200902/fear-failure

Rathvon, N. (1996). *The unmotivated child: Helping your underachiever become a successful student.* New York, NY: Simon and Schuster.

Rayneri, L. J., Gerber, B. L., & Wiley, L. P. (2003). Gifted achievers and gifted underachievers: The impact of learning style preferences in the classroom. *The Journal of Secondary Gifted Education, 14,* 197–204.

Reis, S. M., Burns, D. E., & Renzulli, J. S. (1992). *Curriculum compacting: The complete guide to modifying the regular curriculum for high ability students.* Mansfield Center, CT: Creative Learning Press.

Reis, S. M., Hébert, T. P., Diaz, E. P., Maxfield, L. R., & Ratley, M. E. (1995). *Case studies of talented students who achieve and underachieve in an urban high school* (Research Monograph 95120). Storrs: University of Connecticut, The National Research Center on the Gifted and Talented.

Reis, S. M., & McCoach, D. B. (2000). The underachievement of gifted students: What do we know and where do we go? *Gifted Child Quarterly, 44,* 158–170.

Reis, S. M., Westberg, K. L., Kulikowich, J., Caillard, F., Hébert, T., Plucker, J., . . . Smist, J. M. (1993). *Why not let high ability students start school in January? The curriculum compacting study* (Research Monograph 93106). Storrs: University of Connecticut, The National Research Center on the Gifted and Talented.

Renzulli, J. S. (1982). What makes a problem real: Stalking the illusive meaning of qualitative differences in gifted education. *Gifted Child Quarterly, 26,* 147–156.

Renzulli, J. S. (2005). The Three-Ring Conception of Giftedness: A developmental model for promoting creative productivity. In R. J. Sternberg & J. E. Davidson (Eds.), *Conceptions of giftedness* (2nd ed., pp. 246–279). New York, NY: Cambridge University Press.

Renzulli, J. S. (2012). A theory of giftedness based on the anticipated social roles of high potential youth. In R. F. Subotnik, A. Robinson, C. M. Callahan, & E. J. Gubbins (Eds.), *Malleable minds: Translating insights from psychology and neuroscience to gifted education* (pp. 119–139). Storrs: University of Connecticut, The National Research Center on the Gifted and Talented.

Renzulli, J. S., Reid, B. D., & Gubbins, E. J. (1991). *Setting an agenda: Research priorities for the gifted and talented through the year 2000.* Storrs: University of Connecticut, The National Research Center on the Gifted and Talented.

Renzulli, J. S., & Reis, S. M. (1997). *The Schoolwide Enrichment Model: A how-to guide for educational excellence* (2nd ed.). Mansfield Center, CT: Creative Learning Press.

Rice, K. G., Ashby, J. S., & Preusser, K. J. (1996). Perfectionism, relationships with parents, and self-esteem. *Individual Psychology, 52*, 246–260.

Richert, E. S. (1991). Patterns of underachievement among gifted students. In J. H. Borland (Series Ed.), & M. Bireley & J. Genshaft (Vol. Eds.), *Understanding the gifted adolescent* (pp. 139–162). New York, NY: Teacher College Press.

Rimm, S. (1995). *Why bright kids get poor grades and what you can do about it.* New York, NY: Crown Trade Paperbacks.

Rimm, S. (1996). *Dr. Sylvia Rimm's smart parenting: How to parent so children will learn.* New York, NY: Three Rivers Press.

Rimm, S. (1997). Underachievement syndrome: A national epidemic. In N. Colangelo & G. A. Davis (Eds.), *Handbook of gifted education* (2nd ed., pp. 416–435). Boston, MA: Allyn & Bacon.

Rimm, S. (2008). *Why bright kids get poor grades and what you can do about it: A six-step program for parents and teachers* (3rd ed.). Scottsdale, AZ: Great Potential Press.

Rimm, S., & Lowe, B. (1988). Family environments of underachieving gifted students. *Gifted Child Quarterly, 32*, 353–358.

Rimm, S., Siegle, D., & McCoach, D. B. (2011, November). *Mini keynote—Connecting for high potential: How parents, teachers, and school counselors can work collaboratively to reverse underachievement for gifted students.* Paper presented at the 58th annual convention of the National Association for Gifted Children, New Orleans, LA.

Rimm, S. B. (1986). *Underachievement syndrome: Causes and cures.* Watertown, WI: Apple.

Rimm, S. B. (2003). Underachievement: A national epidemic. In N. Colangelo & G. A. Davis (Eds.), *The handbook of gifted education* (3rd ed., pp. 424–443). Boston, MA: Allyn & Bacon.

Rivero, L. (2010). *A parent's guide to gifted teens: Living with intense and creative adolescents.* Scottsdale, AZ: Great Potential Press.

Ruban, L., & Reis, S. M. (2006). Patterns of self-regulation: Patterns of self-regulatory strategy use among low-achieving and high-achieving university students. *Roeper Review, 28,* 148–156.

Rubenstein, L. D., Siegle, D., Reis, S. M., McCoach, D. B., & Burton, M. G. (2012). A complex quest: The development and research of underachievement interventions for gifted students. *Psychology in the Schools, 49,* 678–694.

Sanders, M. G. (1998). The effects of school, family, and community support on the academic achievement of African American adolescents. *Urban Education, 33,* 385–409.

Schuler, P. A. (2000). Perfectionism and gifted adolescents. *The Journal of Secondary Gifted Education, 11,* 183–196.

Schunk, D. H. (1981). Modeling and attributional effects on children's achievement: A self-efficacy analysis. *Journal of Educational Psychology, 73,* 93–105.

Schunk, D. H. (1984). Sequential attributional feedback and children's achievement behaviors. *Journal of Educational Psychology, 75,* 511–518.

Schunk, D. H. (1989a). Self-efficacy and cognitive achievement: Implications for students with learning problems. *Journal of Learning Disabilities, 22,* 14–22.

Schunk, D. H. (1989b). Self-efficacy and cognitive skill learning. In C. Ames & R. Ames (Eds.), *Research on motivation in education* (pp. 13–44). San Diego, CA: Academic Press.

Schunk, D. H., & Hanson, A. R. (1985). Peer models: Influence on children's self-efficacy and achievement. *Journal of Educational Psychology, 77,* 313–322.

Schunk, D. H., & Hanson, A. R. (1989). Self-modeling and children's cognitive skill learning. *Journal of Educational Psychology, 81,* 155–163.

Schunk, D. H., & Rice, J. M. (1984, August). *Strategy self-verbalization: Effects on remedial readers' comprehension and self-efficacy.* Paper presented at the annual meeting of the American Psychological Association, Toronto, Canada.

Sheard, M. (2009). Hardiness commitment, gender, and age differentiate university academic performance. *British Journal of Educational Psychology, 79,* 189–204.

Siegle, D. (2007, September). Gifted children's bill of rights. *Parenting for High Potential, 3,* 30.

Siegle, D. (2008). The time is now to stand up for gifted education: 2007 NAGC Presidential Address. *Gifted Child Quarterly, 52,* 111–113.

Siegle, D. (2012, April). *Research related to the Achievement Orientation Model as it relates to underachievement of gifted students.* Paper presented at the annual meeting of the American Educational Research Association, Vancouver, BC.

Siegle, D., & McCoach, D. B. (2005a). Making a difference: Motivating gifted students who are not achieving. *TEACHING Exceptional Children, 38*(1), 22–27.

Siegle, D., & McCoach, D. B. (2005b). *Motivating gifted students.* Waco, TX: Prufrock Press.

Siegle, D., & McCoach, D. B. (2007). Increasing student mathematics self-efficacy through teacher training. *Journal of Advanced Academics, 18,* 278–312.

Siegle, D., & McCoach, D. B. (in press). Underachieving gifted students. In C. M. Callahan & H. Hertberg-Davis (Eds.), *Fundamentals of gifted education.* New York, NY: Taylor & Francis.

Siegle, D., & Reis, S. M. (1998). Gender differences in teacher and student perceptions of gifted students' ability. *Gifted Child Quarterly, 42,* 39–48.

Siegle, D., Reis, S. M., & McCoach, D. B. (2006, June). *A study to increase academic achievement among gifted underachievers.* Poster presented at the 2006 Institute of Education Sciences Research Conference, Washington, DC.

Siegle, D., Rubenstein, L. D., & McCoach, D. B. (2011, April). *Comparing teachers', parents', and gifted underachieving students' personal perceptions of factors associated with student achievement.* Paper presented at the annual meeting of the American Educational Research Association, New Orleans, LA.

Siegle, D., Rubenstein, L. D., & Mitchell, M. S. (2010, May). *Honors students' perceptions of their high school experiences: A validation of best practices in gifted education.* Paper presented at the 2010 annual meeting of the American Education Research Association, Denver, CO.

Siegle, D., Rubenstein, L. D., Pollard, E., & Romey, E. (2010). Exploring the relationship of college freshman honors students' effort and ability attribution, interest, and implicit theory of intelligence with perceived ability. *Gifted Child Quarterly, 54,* 92–101.

Skaalvik, E. M., & Skaalvik, S. (2004). Self-concept and self-efficacy: A test of the internal/external frame of reference model and predictions of subsequent motivation and achievement. *Psychological Reports, 95,* 1187–1202.

Speirs Neumeister, K. (2010). Perfectionism in gifted children. *KAGE Update,* Issue 3, 1, 9–10.

Speirs Neumeister, K. L. (2004). Understanding the relationship between perfectionism and achievement motivation in gifted college students. *Gifted Child Quarterly, 48,* 219–231.

Speirs Neumeister, K. L., & Finch, H. (2006). Perfectionism in high-ability students: Relational precursors and influences on achievement motivation. *Gifted Child Quarterly, 50,* 238–251.

Speirs Neumeister, K. L., Williams, K. K., & Cross, T. L. (2009). Gifted high-school students' perspectives on the development of perfectionism. *Roeper Review, 31,* 198–206.

Starko, A. J. (1986). *It's about time: Inservice strategies for curriculum compacting.* Mansfield Center, CT: Creative Learning Press.

Steele, C. (2000, September). *Promoting educational success: Social and cultural considerations.* Paper presented at the U.S. Department of Education and The National Academies' Millennium Conference, Achieving High Educational Standards for All, Washington, DC.

Sternberg, R. J. (2001, July). *Successful intelligence.* Paper presented at the annual Edufest Institute, Boise, ID.

Sternberg, R. J., & Davidson, J. E. (2005). *Conceptions of giftedness* (2nd ed.). New York, NY: Cambridge University Press.

Stevens, T., Olivárez, A., Jr., & Hamman, D. (2006). The role of cognition, motivation, and emotion in explaining the mathematics achievement gap between Hispanic and White students. *Hispanic Journal of Behavioral Sciences, 28,* 161–186.

Strayhorn, J. (2003). *Cognitive restructuring.* Retrieved from http://www.psyskills.com/cogther01.htm

Stroessner, S., Good, C., & Webster, L. (n.d.). *What can be done to reduce stereotype threat?* Retrieved from http://reducing stereotypethreat.org

Subotnik, R. F., Olszewski-Kubilius, P., & Worrell, F. C. (2011). Rethinking giftedness and gifted education: A proposed direction forward based on psychological science. *Psychological Science in the Public Interest, 12*(1), 3–54.

Supplee, P. L. (1990). *Reaching the gifted underachiever.* New York, NY: Teacher College Press.

Tannenbaum, A. J. (1962). *Adolescent attitudes toward academic brilliance* (Talented Youth Project monograph). New York, NY: Bureau of Publications, Teachers College, Columbia University.

Taylor, C. W. (1986). Cultivating simultaneous student growth in both multiple creative talents and knowledge. In J. S. Renzulli (Ed.), *Systems and models for developing programs for the gifted and talented* (pp. 306–351). Mansfield Center, CT: Creative Learning Press.

Tomlinson, C. A., Callahan, C. M., & Lelli, K. M. (1997). Challenging expectations: Case studies of culturally diverse young children. *Gifted Child Quarterly, 41,* 5–17.

Torrance, E. P. (1983). *Manifesto for children.* Athens, GA: Georgia Studies of Creative Behavior and Full Circle Counseling.

Usher, E. L., & Pajares, F. (2006). Sources of academic and self-regulatory efficacy beliefs of entering middle school students. *Contemporary Educational Psychology, 31,* 125–141.

Warnemuende, C., & Samson, J. H. (1991). *Underachievement: Reversing the process.* Seal Beach, CA: Family Life.

Weiner, B. (1986). *An attributional theory of motivation and emotion.* New York, NY: Springer-Verlag.

Weiner, B. (1992). *Human motivation: Metaphors, theories, and research.* Newbury Park, CA: SAGE.

Westberg, K. L., Archambault, F. X., Jr., Dobyns, S. M., & Salvin, T. J. (1993). *An observation study of instructional and curricular practices used with gifted and talented students in regular classrooms* (Research Monograph 93104). Storrs: University of Connecticut, The National Research Center on the Gifted and Talented.

White, P. H., Sanbonmatsu, D. M., Croyle, R. T., & Smittipatana, S. (2002). Test of socially motivated underachievement: "Letting up" for others. *Journal of Experimental Social Psychology, 38,* 162–169.

Whitmore, J. R. (1980). *Giftedness, conflict, and underachievement.* Boston, MA: Allyn & Bacon.

Whitmore, J. R. (1986). Understanding a lack of motivation to excel. *Gifted Child Quarterly, 30,* 66–69.

Wigfield, A., & Eccles, J. S. (2000). Expectancy-value theory of achievement motivation. *Contemporary Educational Psychology, 25,* 68–81.

Wood, R. E., & Locke, E. A. (1987). The relationship of self-efficacy and grade goals to academic performance. *Educational and Psychological Measurement, 47,* 1013–1024.

Worrell, F. C. (2007). Ethnic identity, academic achievement, and global self-concept in four groups of academically talented adolescents. *Gifted Child Quarterly, 51,* 23–38.

Wyner, J. S., Bridgeland, J. M., & DiIulio, J. J., Jr. (2007). *Achievement trap: How America is failing millions of high-achieving students from lower-income families.* Retrieved from http://www.jkcf.org/assets/files/0000/0084/Achievement_Trap.pdf

Yu, S. (1996). *Cognitive strategy use and motivation in underachieving students* (Unpublished doctoral dissertation). University of Michigan, Ann Arbor.

Zilli, M. G. (1971). Reasons why the gifted adolescent underachieves and some of the implications of guidance and counseling to this problem. *Gifted Child Quarterly, 15,* 279–292.

Zimmerman, B. J., Bonner, S., & Kovach, R. (1996). *Developing self-regulated learners: Beyond achievement to self-efficacy.* Washington, DC: American Psychological Association.

Zimmerman, B. J., & Martinez-Pons, M. (1990). Student differences in self-regulated learning: Relating grade, sex, and giftedness to self-efficacy and strategy use. *Journal of Educational Psychology, 82,* 51–59.

The National Association for Gifted Children's Position Paper on Giftedness

Redefining Giftedness for a New Century: Shifting the Paradigm

Gifted individuals are those who demonstrate outstanding levels of aptitude (defined as an exceptional ability to reason and learn) or competence (documented performance or achievement in top 10% or rarer) in one or more domains. Domains include any structured area of activity with its own symbol system (e.g., mathematics, music, language) and/or set of sensorimotor skills (e.g., painting, dance, sports).

The development of ability or talent is a lifelong process. It can be evident in young children as exceptional performance on tests and/or other measures of ability or as a rapid rate of learning, compared to other students of the same age, or in actual achievement in a domain. As individuals mature through childhood to adolescence, however, achievement and high levels of motivation in the domain become the primary characteristics of their giftedness. Various factors can either enhance or inhibit the development and expression of abilities.

Implications for Educators. Exceptionally capable learners are children who progress in learning at a significantly faster pace than do other children of the same age, often resulting in high levels of achievement. Such children are found in all segments of society. Beginning in early childhood, their optimal development requires differentiated educational experiences, both of a general nature and, increasingly over time, targeting those domains in which they demonstrate the capacity for high levels of performance. Such differentiated educational experiences consist of adjustments in the level, depth, and pacing of curriculum and outside-of-school programs to match their current levels of achievement and learning rates. Marked differences among gifted learners sometimes require additional and unusual interventions. Additional support services include more comprehensive assessment, counseling, parent education, and specially designed programs, including those typically afforded older students.

Barriers to attainment. Some gifted individuals with exceptional aptitude may not demonstrate outstanding levels of achievement due to environmental circumstances such as limited opportunities to learn as a result of poverty, discrimination, or cultural barriers; due to physical or learning disabilities; or due to motivational or emotional problems. Identification of these students will need to emphasize aptitude rather than relying only on demonstrated achievement. Such students will need challenging programs and additional support services if they are to develop their ability and realize optimal levels of performance.

Adulthood. As individuals transition to appropriate higher education and specialized training, and eventually to independence, they will profit from targeted guidance and support. Continuing high levels of exceptional adult performance will require, in addition to advanced knowledge and skills, high levels of motivation, perseverance, and creative problem-solving. Exceptionally capable adults are among those most likely to contribute to the advancement of a society and its scientific, humanistic, and social goals.

Implications for Policy Makers. Policy Makers should be aware that the gifted persons described here will comprise a large proportion of the leadership of the next generation in the arts, sciences, letters, politics, etc. If we provide this group with a mediocre education we doom ourselves to a mediocre society a generation forward. Educators know how to provide an excellent education for these students, but it will not happen by accident or benign neglect.

Policy Makers control the allocation of resources, and trained educators of exceptionally capable students know how to use these resources constructively. These should be brought into alignment to the benefit of all. Does this mean that we tear these scarce resources from other students including those with disabilities or living in troubled circumstance? No, quite the contrary. A moral society must care for and enhance the development of all of its citizens. Specific investment in the gifted is an important way to build a society that can help solve the society's needs with creative innovations and organizations.

Board Approval

Approved by the Board (March 2010). The original content, research, and drafts of this position paper were developed and assembled by individuals with expertise in the area. This final version represents discussions, revisions, and conclusions of the NAGC Board to reflect the national policy position of NAGC.

Author's Note

This position paper was reprinted with permission of the National Association for Gifted Children (http://www.nagc.org).

About the Author

Del Siegle, Ph.D., is a professor in gifted and talented education and Head of the Department of Educational Psychology at the University of Connecticut. Prior to earning his Ph.D., Del worked as a gifted and talented coordinator in Montana. He is a past president of the National Association for Gifted Children and served on the board of directors of The Association for the Gifted. He is coeditor of *Gifted Child Quarterly* and authors a technology column for *Gifted Child Today.* Dr. Siegle is also coauthor with Gary Davis and Sylvia Rimm of the popular textbook, *Education of the Gifted and Talented.* As a former teacher, and now university professor, Dr. Siegle has spent two decades addressing the issue of gifted underachievers.